WRITING DIFFER

*Readings from the seminar
of Hélène Cixous*

GENDER IN WRITING

Series Editor: Kate Flint, Fellow and Tutor in English, Mansfield College, Oxford

Difference in language, in subject matter, in form. This series seeks to explore what is distinctive about women's and men's writing, and to examine the theories of sexuality which attempt to explain these differences. Writings of all periods and genres will be looked at from a variety of radical perspectives: some explicitly feminist, others examining masculinity, homosexuality and gender politics as they are constructed through the writing and reading of texts. The series will draw on recent developments in literary theory in order to examine all aspects of gender in writing.

WRITING DIFFERENCES
Readings from the seminar
of Hélène Cixous

Edited by
SUSAN SELLERS

OPEN UNIVERSITY PRESS
MILTON KEYNES

Open University Press
Open University Educational Enterprises Limited
12 Cofferidge Close
Stony Stratford
Milton Keynes MK11 1BY

First published 1988

British Library Cataloguing in Publication Data

Writing differences: readings from the
  seminar of Hélène Cixous.——(Gender in
  writing series).
  1. Sex differences (Psychology) in
  literature
  I. Sellers, Susan   II. Cixous, Hélène
  III. Series
  809'.93353   PN56.S52

  ISBN 0–335–09010–9
  ISBN 0–335–09009–5 Pbk

Typeset by Quadra Graphics, Oxford
Printed in Great Britain by the Alden Press, Oxford

For Marguerite Sandré

'J'avais essayé de le lire et je n'avais rien compris. C'était donc là que je devais aller.'

Contents

Acknowledgements		ix
Contributors		xi
1	Introduction	1
	Susan Sellers	
2	Extreme fidelity	9
	Hélène Cixous	
3	Tancredi continues	37
	Hélène Cixous	
4	Let's go to the fountain: on George Sand and writing	54
	Anne Berger	
5	Crossing the mirror to the forbidden land (Lewis Carroll's *Alice in Wonderland* and Marina Tsvetaeva's 'The Devil'	66
	Mara Négron Marreo	
6	Visions of life's tempest: from Shakespeare to Karen Blixen	71
	Nadia Setti	
7	Djuna Barnes' *Nightwood*: where man is with wo(e)	81
	Mairéad Hanrahan	
8	Jean Genet's *The Miracle of the Rose*	95
	Violette Santellani	
9	Spinning form: reading Clarice Lispector	98
	Regina Helena de Oliveira Machado	
10	Hélène Cixous' *Ou l'art de l'innocence*: the path to you	113
	Pierre Salesne	
11	Hélène Cixous' *Le Livre de Promethea*: paradise refound	127
	Sarah Cornell	

Contents

12 Conversations with Hélène Cixous and members of the Centre   141
   d'Etudes Féminines
   Selected further reading   155
   Books by Hélène Cixous   157

Acknowledgements

The editor and contributors wish to acknowledge:
Carcanet Press for quotation from Giovanni Pontiero's translations of
The Foreign Legion and *The Hour of the Star*; Editions des femmes for
translation from *Ou l'art de l'innocence*; Editora do Autor for translation
from *A Paixão Segundo G.H.*; Editora Nova Fronteira for translation from
'Tanta Mansidão'; *Etudes Freudiennes* for translation of 'Tancrède
continue'; Faber and Faber Ltd and Farrar Straus: Giroux for quotation
from *Nightwood*; Editions Gallimard for quotation and translation from
Le Livre de Promethea; Penguin Books and University of Chicago Press
for quotation from 'Tempests' in *Anecdotes of Destiny*, copyright © Isak
Dinesen, 1958; Virago Press for quotation from J. Martin King's
translation of *A Captive Spirit* (Marina Tsvetaeva), copyright © 1980 by
Ardis; The University of Chicago Press for quotations from 'Peter and
Rosa' in *Winter's Tales*.

The editor would also like to thank Kate Flint for her help in revising
the final typescript.

Note on Translation

In accordance with the practice of the seminar, the written translations
for this volume have tried to remain as close to the structure of the
original language as possible.

Contributors

Anne Berger is of French nationality. She is a specialist in 19th-century French poetry and is currently visiting lecturer in French at the University of Cornell. She has published on Rimbaud and George Sand and is an adviser to the journal *Diacritics*.

Hélène Cixous was born in Oran in Algeria of French and German parentage. She is Professor of Literature at the experimental University of Paris VIII–Vincennes and the director of the Centre d'Etudes Féminines which she founded in 1974. She is author of over thirty books, numerous articles and essays, and several radio and stage plays.

Sarah Cornell, born in Springfield, Ohio, USA, graduated with an MA from New York University. She is currently completing a doctoral thesis on Hélène Cixous for the Centre d'Etudes Féminines. She has been a member of the research seminar since 1976.

Mairéad Hanrahan was born in southern Ireland and graduated with joint honours in French and economics from University College, Dublin. She is currently completing her doctoral thesis on sexual identity in Djuna Barnes and Jean Genet in conjunction with the centre d'Etudes Féminines.

Ann Liddle was born in Wisconsin, USA, where, after extensive periods of living and travelling abroad, she returned to take an MA in French literature. She joined Hélène Cixous' seminar in 1977 to continue research on translation.

Regina Helena de Oliveira Machado was born in Brazil. She studied ethnology at the University of São Paulo before coming to Paris to complete a doctoral thesis on the work of Clarice Lispector. She has translated two of Lispector's texts into French for the Editions des femmes.

Mara Négron Marreo feels that the continuing existence of the rhythms of the Spanish language on the US dominated island of Puerto Rico bears testimony to the miracle of human resistance. Her passport certifies her as 'American' since her Puertorican nationality has been declared 'illegal'. She has a BA from the University of Puerto Rico and is currently in the final stages of doctoral research on 'feminine knowledge' which will include reference to the work of George Sand and Clarice Lispector.

Pierre Salesne is of French nationality and has been a member of the research seminar since its foundation in 1974. He has worked principally on Hélène Cixous, Kleist and Hofmannsthal. Together with Anne Berger, Sarah Cornell, Mara Négron Marreo, Marguerite Sandré and Nadia Setti, he is an editor of the Paris revue *Fruits*.

Marguerite Sandré, to whom this volume is dedicated, describes herself as the 'grandmother' of the seminar. After a full teaching career she joined the seminar first as a member of its audience. In addition to her active participation in its ongoing research, she has remained to become the seminar's secretary, archivist and general co-ordinator.

Violette Santellani was born in the south of France where she completed her MA studies to become a teacher of literature and history. She has worked as a member of the research seminar since 1982. She completed her first novel in 1984 and is currently working on her second. The arrival of her baby daughter, Lys, coincided with the birth of the present volume.

Susan Sellers has degrees from the University of London and the Sorbonne and has worked with the Centre d'Etudes Féminines since 1983. Her lecturing and research assignments have taken her as far afield as Africa and South America. She has published articles on French feminism and the work of Hélène Cixous and is author of *Language and Sexual Difference: Feminist Writing in France* (Macmillan 1988).

Nadia Setti was born in Modena in northern Italy. She completed her BA thesis at the University of Rome on narrative structure in Sterne's *Tristram Shandy*, which she followed with a year's postgraduate study in Belgium. She took her doctoral thesis with the Centre d'Etudes Féminines on the feminine subject in Virginia Woolf, Marguerite Duras and Hélène Cixous in 1983.

1

Introduction

Susan Sellers

The Centre d'Etudes Féminines was founded by Hélène Cixous as part of the experimental University of Paris VIII–Vincennes in 1974. The essays contained in this volume have been commissioned from Hélène Cixous and other members of her research seminar to illustrate the Centre's pioneering work on sexual difference and its relationship to the literary text.

The question of gender is central to the definition of a feminine mode of research. Hélène Cixous' adoption of the term 'feminine' derives from the description of a particular type of response to the laws which govern patriarchy. Cixous draws on Freud's theory of the Oedipal process to posit two different poles of responding to patriarchal law. Arguing against the rejection of Freudian psychoanalysis current in feminism, Cixous finds in Freud's account a useful model for the process by which the amorphic, desire-driven human infant is socialized to assume its adult role.

In her introductory text 'Extreme fidelity', Cixous illustrates the classic response to patriarchal law as that of submission. Like the countryman of Kafka's short story who spends his entire life waiting before the law, she shows how the tendency is to accept its supremacy, interiorizing the threat of castration to remain circumscribed within its shadow. Cixous contrasts the countryman's response with that of Eve in the garden of Eden. The French philosopher Jacques Derrida has demonstrated how Western thinking is founded in the myth of an originary first term or 'logos', and Cixous shows how an attentive reading of the biblical scene highlights the functioning of this myth. Three properties of the law become apparent. Not only is the law a word, but it is a word which has no meaning since death does not exist in the paradisal state. Finally, the law has a relationship to both knowledge and pleasure. Though the biblical patriarchs have laid the blame for the loss of Paradise at Eve's door, Cixous sees Eve's decision to follow her desire and refusal to grant the law its power as having other interpretations.

Cixous labels Eve's response to the law 'feminine' in order to distinguish it from the classic 'masculine' response. She believes that the two scenes symbolize the way all of us are required to deal with social schema. We can choose to accept their prohibitions, or, like Eve, we can ignore and defy the law, searching for the means to inscribe our defiance in the attempt to subvert its power.

In her second essay 'Tancredi continues', Hélène Cixous cites the example of the famous lovers to illustrate how the potential for 'masculine' and 'feminine' is present in both sexes. She shows how our gender identities are not fixed to one pole or another, but mediate between them over a fluctuating and wide range of possibilities. Indeed, while a 'feminine' position is privileged as the way forward for women *and* men, the pure adoption of this position is shown to be both untenable and undesirable. In the same way that the interdiction of phallic law forces the infant to recognize others' needs and desires, so elements of 'masculinity' are required to ensure the provision of 'order' and the imposition of necessary limits.

Insistence on the 'feminine' as a position open to both men and women does not, however, mean the denial of biological sex differences. In 'Extreme fidelity', Hélène Cixous explains that if she chooses the terms 'masculine' and 'feminine', it is because they have a grounding in cultural fact. She argues that because of the way society has used sexual difference, women remain closer to a 'feminine economy' than men, and that it is women who must initiate the changes that will revolutionize social and political order.[1]

In the text entitled 'Conversations', Hélène Cixous argues that the biological differences between the sexes give rise to different bodily experiences, and thus create different sources of knowledge. While these 'sexual' experiences are only a small part of the experience of being human, Cixous shows how they involve different perceptions, and contain the potential for different metaphors of understanding.

Cixous' insistence on sexual difference is symptomatic of a valuing of differences of all kinds. This valuing stems from recognition of the fundamental role of difference, in language, thought, and the construction of group and self identity. Linguistically, structuralism has shown how it is the differences between signifiers that generates meaning, while the hierarchical ordering of difference is recognized as the fulcrum of philosophic thinking.[2] In the psychoanalytic account of the construction of self-identity, it is perception of difference which activates the infant's awareness of itself as distinct from the (M)other; while such pioneering studies as the French historian Michel Foucault's *The Order of Things* have identified the acknowledgement and articulation of difference as the organizing principle underlying the formation of all social groups.[3]

Implicit in the positioning of the 'logos' as unchallenged first term is its imposition of its definition of difference on all succeeding terms. Countering the appropriation endemic to the successful functioning of the phallus, Cixous calls for a new attitude to difference which will involve 'feminine' acceptance of whatever is recognized as 'other'. Recent developments in psychoanalytic theory have emphasized the impossibility of creating a fixed ego-identity, and Derrida's work on deconstruction has led to revision of the essentially stable structuralist premise that meaning is a result of the differences between signifiers, to include a reverberating play of both present and absent differences along an entire linguistic chain. Cixous urges recognition of the multiple nature of the self which can never simplify itself to conform to the illusion of its unified mirror image. She calls for new forms of definition which do not depend on mastery, which accept 'chaos', and value and celebrate difference. In 'Extreme fidelity' Cixous writes 'it is in poetic writing that something of the mystery and continuity of life can appear, through grammatical subversion, through a certain liberty taken inside language, with regard to the law of gender'. As the content and structure of the essays in this volume make clear, literature is intrinsic to this search for 'feminine' modes of giving form.

In line with the post-structuralist emphasis on language, the French psychoanalyst Jacques Lacan has rewritten Freudian theory to highlight the role of language in the Oedipal process. Lacan has redrawn Freud's model to show how severance from the (M)other entails the infant's need to symbolize what is thereby constituted as other. The passage from the 'imaginary' state of symbiotic dependence on the (M)other, to the 'symbolic' stage of ego definition and control, is thus seen to be concomitant with the acquisition of language.

Anne Berger's essay on George Sand explores this passage from the 'imaginary' to the 'symbolic'. Taking the quotation 'Let's go to the fountain' as her title, she shows how critical studies of George Sand's work have over-simplified or misinterpreted Sand's assumption of a male identity. She examines George Sand's autobiography and the series of country life novels to show how the adoption of a 'son's' persona originates in a complex network of associations that focus on the mother. Anne Berger follows both Lacan's and Julia Kristeva's account of the catastrophic separation from an originary 'mother tongue', but argues that Sand's revolutionary vision is to see the ensuing 'coming to speech' as 'the gift of transference' of the mother's love. In contrast to the repression of primary sources of communication fashionable in current psychoanalytic theory, Berger demonstrates how a re-reading of George Sand's work reveals new insights into the maternal role, as the pleasure the infant derives from this primary source extends into the mature pleasure of artistic creation.

Anne Berger describes with reference to George Sand's own life how the lessons of 'education' — the lessons which repress primary, maternal patterns of communication — have to be unlearned, and this is a theme which is continued in Mara Négron Marreo's reading of Lewis Carroll's *Alice in Wonderland* and Marina Tsvetaeva's short story 'The Devil'. Mara Négron Marreo shows how in the imaginary worlds of 'Wonderland' and 'the devil's room', there is a return to the pre-symbolic order in which bodily contact is the only means of knowing the world. As in Anne Berger's essay, this emphasis on the primacy of bodily sources is not seen as a regression, but as a link back to the maternal, providing a way round the inevitable exile into the symbolic. 'Wonderland' and 'the devil's room' reflect the primary scene of exile, which is symbolized in the two stories through references to the biblical version in Eden. Seen through a mirror, the established order is inverted, and instead of interdiction there is invitation. Accepting the invitation transports both Alice and Tsvetaeva's heroine beyond the one-sided world of 'before the mirror', where reflection is part of the struggle for self-possession, where knowledge is caught in the hierarchy of binary oppositions, and language has to be mastered. Like the games originating in cards played by both Alice and Musya, the new order is one in which recourse to the maternal is the prerequisite for the pleasure to be derived from the new potential of the symbolic, giving rise in the case of Tsvetaeva to the language of poetry.

The mirror image is repeated in Nadia Setti's essay on 'Tempests'. In her introductory discussion of the tempest in *King Lear*, Setti shows how, at the beginning of the play, Lear's search for flattering confirmation of his royal image takes precedence over his feelings as a father. Nadia Setti goes on to illustrate how it takes the experience of the tempest to undermine Lear's 'masculinity', for Lear to learn to take notice of others, and confront without evasion the truth of the human condition. 'The tempest' can thus be read as the metaphor of a force capable of overturning history, breaking down barriers and distinctions, and creating the necessary conditions for reassessment. Setti traces the metaphor through Shakespeare's *Tempest* to a short story by Karen Blixen about a production of the play. She shows how in Karen Blixen's story, the main character undergoes the dramatic as well as a real experience of tempest, to finally abandon her dream of an imaginary love union with a fairy-tale 'prince'.

Towards the end of Karen Blixen's 'Tempests', the heroine writes a poem in which she describes and then transforms her sense of loss at the abandonment of her fairy-tale dream. This vision, which enables the heroine to reject the illusion of final definition, and accept the tempestuous disorder of life, is a far cry from the experience of Djuna Barnes' *Nightwood*.

In her reading of *Nightwood*, Mairéad Hanrahan highlights the characters' desperate search for 'form' as the mainspring of the book's momentum. In contrast to the country life novels of George Sand where love is seen as a maieutic force capable of giving birth to the self, Mairéad Hanrahan shows how in *Nightwood* love is held responsible for humanity's 'carnivorous' desire to possess and 'devour' the other. In the tortured universe of the novel, being in love means the possibility of an identity through the adoption of the form given by another. Hanrahan shows how even the sexually indeterminate Robin, who at first seems to lack the torturous desire that activates the other characters, and therefore to be exempt from the agony of the human predicament, is brought by 'love' to join their futile search. At the opposite pole to Karen Blixen's story, *Nightwood* illustrates the destruction that results when the search for a 'masculine' subjectivity becomes the goal of both sexes.

In her short text on Jean Genet's *The Miracle of the Rose*, Violette Santellani explores the masculine, homosexual universe of a prison to show how femininity may be discovered in the most unlikely source. She traces its textual inscription in relation to the child murderer Harcamone, to discover its final blossoming as Harcamone mounts the scaffold to die. Her contribution presents a close textual analysis of the selected passage, and illustrates a poetic response to the experience of reading.

At the end of her essay on *Nightwood*, Mairéad Hanrahan speculates as to the reason for the twenty-year gap between the writing of this novel and Djuna Barnes' next work, wondering whether Barnes' attempt to give textual form to her suffering had only served to render her experience more painful. Writing as the 'giving of form' is the theme of Regina de Oliveira Machado's text on Clarice Lispector.

Referring to Clarice Lispector's *A Paixão segundo G.H. (The Passion according to G.H.)*, Regina de Oliveira Machado's essay focuses on the section in which the central character, G.H., is brought to acknowledge the existence of the other and to a new assessment of herself through her discovery of the maid's room. Studying the hieroglyphic inscriptions of the maid's drawing on the wall, G.H.'s failure to take notice of the maid is forced to the surface as she becomes aware of the maid's reading of her. Deciphering the other's inscription, G.H. is confronted with aspects of herself that challenge the social, sexual and professional identity she has sought to establish.

Regina de Oliveira Machado shows how the writing of *G.H.* is the 'giving of form' to G.H.'s experience, Clarice Lispector's attempt to understand, organize and express G.H.'s story. At the same time,

Machado shows how throughout Lispector's work there is recognition that writing must respect experience, preserving its 'otherness', without neutralizing or destroying it through the attempted integration of authorial 'understanding'. Machado shows how *A Paixão segundo G.H.* represents the first movement of a process of 'deheroization' which increasingly marks Lispector's later texts. She describes how these final texts are spun from the fragments left by the author's refusal to impose 'form', incorporating threads of 'incomprehension' and even silence in their textual weave.

This refusal to impose upon the other in order to gratify the self has led Hélène Cixous to describe Clarice Lispector's work as the outstanding illustration of 'feminine' writing. In Pierre Salesne's essay, one of Cixous's own texts — *Ou l'art de l'innocence (Or the Art of Innocence)* — is read as an example of 'feminine' writing.

In his essay, Pierre Salesne traces the author's search for a writing position of 'innocence'. This position is not the naive innocence of ignorance, but the hard to achieve 'innocence' of a refusal of mastery. Salesne shows how this search involves the author in the creation of a new type of literary text. Rejecting the phallic structure of traditional literary discourse, its movement is metonymic, resembling what he takes to be the organic evolution of music. Pierre Salesne describes 'feminine' writing as that which originates in the writing 'body' of the author. He shows how *Ou l'art de l'innocence* is a writing that 'gives birth' — not to the authorially crafted characters of traditional literature, but to the multiple potential selves of the writing I.

Pierre Salesne suggests that this early emphasis on the writing I gives place in Cixous' later texts to the 'naming' of 'you'. It is a point which is developed in Sarah Cornell's close textual reading of an opening sequence from *Le Livre de Promethea (The Book of Promethea)*. As in *Ou l'art de l'innocence*, the author rejects conventional narrative structures since these would deform the 'otherness' of Promethea. Sarah Cornell illustrates how, in Cixous' early work, writing is adopted as a transgressive means of creating an entry *back* into 'paradise', while in *Le Livre de Promethea*, the function of the writing alters to become a means of living the '*present* paradise' of a love relationship. The fictional problem is no longer a working through of the anxieties attendant upon realization of the impossibility of being in control, but one of ordering the 'ensemble of present moments' of the relationship with Promethea. Cornell shows how in *Le Livre de Promethea* there is a splitting of the authorial I, as the writer allows herself to be transported as both living and writing subject beyond the ego's search for mastery, to encounter Promethea.

In the text entitled 'Conversations' with which this volume ends, Hélène Cixous confirms this movement in her writing, beyond the 'inaugural' stages of self-preoccupation to explicit 'political' concern. She presents a resumé of her writing career, and details the aims and practices of 'études féminines' as exemplified by the research seminar.

In 'Conversations', Hélène Cixous emphasizes that the (sexual, linguistic and other) differences that characterize the seminar are intrinsic to a 'feminine' mode of research. She describes 'feminine' research as the study of different responses to the fundamental conditions of life. She endorses her belief in the value of literature as the site of the inscription of these differences, and describes how 'feminine' writing presents radical alternatives to the appropriation and destruction of difference necessitated by phallic law.

A 'feminine' mode of research also has implications for the way a text is approached. Reading becomes an act of listening. The application of textual theories which serve to confirm the superior position of the reader is resisted, for the adoption of a state of 'active receptivity' in which the reader tries to 'hear' what the text is consciously and unconsciously saying. Hélène Cixous explains how 'listening' to the text involves stringent work on the self. She uses the metaphor of a visit to a foreign country to show how a reader will select those elements which correspond to his or her individual questions, needs and desires. A 'feminine' reading acknowledges these predilections as its starting point. Though no reading can ever be definitive, a reading which 'opens' itself in this way will, Cixous believes, lead the reader to awareness of other possible threads, enabling the reader to advance further on the path of textual and self-understanding.

In the same way that the attempt to value difference involves the search for the 'right distance' to the other, so a relationship to the text which seeks to preserve its otherness requires constant readjustment. Cixous explains how a 'feminine' reading may mean the adoption of a whole range of textual perspectives, and details the alternative organiza-tional practices that such an approach to the text entails. She emphasizes the importance of working collectively, stressing that — unlike the judgemental hierarchy of patriarchal institutions — a 'feminine' collecti-vity is founded on the multiplicity of readings that bring a text into play. The range of essays in this volume, which span a broad spectrum of research experience, reflects this collective approach.

Hélène Cixous concludes 'Conversations' with a renewed emphasis on the importance of 'poetic' thinking. She explains her suspicion of 'party politics', calling for a new, 'feminine' approach to politics grounded in respect for the other. Thus the feminist problematic of the personal and the political might be posed in a new way. 'Learning to love the other' will, Cixous believes, not only mean changes in our sexual and social relationships, but will also bring about corresponding changes in cultural and political order.[4] 'Poetic' language — because it breaks free

from the rules that govern phallic discourse, because it leaves space for
the other, and because it continually searches to inscribe meanings in
new ways — would be the locus of such a revolution. The essays
collected in this volume have been written from the basis of this
conviction.

Notes

1. See, for example, Hélène Cixous' 'The laugh of the Medusa', in Isabelle de
   Courtivron and Elaine Marks (eds), *New French Feminisms*, Brighton, Harvester, 1981, translated by Keith Cohen and Paula Cohen, pp. 245–64. (This essay
   is a revised version of 'Le Rire de la Méduse' in *L'Arc*, no. 61, Paris, 1975,
   pp. 39–54.)
2. See, for example, Hélène Cixous' 'Sorties' in *La Jeune Née*, with Catherine
   Clément, Paris, Union Générale d'Editions, Collection 10/18, 1977, pp. 115–
   246. An extract from this essay has been translated by Ann Liddle in *New
   French Feminisms*, pp. 90–98.
3. Michel Foucault, *Les Mots et les choses: une archéologie des sciences humaines*, Paris,
   Gallimard, 1966. The English translation is *The Order of Things: An Archaeology
   of the Human Sciences*, London, 1974.
4. See, for example, Hélène Cixous' 'La Venue à l'écriture', in *La Venue à
   l'écriture* with Catherine Clément and Madeleine Gagnon, Paris, Union
   Générale d'Editions, Collection 10/18, 1977, (reprinted in *Entre l'écriture*,
   Editions des femmes, Paris, 1986, pp. 9–69).

2

Extreme fidelity

Hélène Cixous

Translated from the French by Ann Liddle
and Susan Sellers

(The following text is based on a lecture given by Hélène
Cixous to the International College of Philosophy in Paris on
28 January 1984. The lecture has been revised by Hélène
Cixous with a new introduction and conclusion for publication
in the present volume.)

I have always dreamed about the last text of a great writer. A text written
with final energies, the last breath. On the last day before death, the
author sits on the edge of the earth, feet light in the infinite air, and looks
at the stars. Tomorrow the author will be a star among the stars, a
molecule among all the molecules. The last day is beautiful for those
who know how to live it, it is one of the most beautiful days of life. On
that particular day (I should say days, for the last day can be several days)
one sees the world with the eye of the Gods: I am finally going to
become a part of the worldy mysteries. Sitting on the edge of the earth
the author is already almost no one. The phrases which come from the
heart to the lips are released from the book. They are beautiful like the
work, but they will never be published, and before the imminence of the
starred silence, they hasten, assemble, and say the essential. They are a
sublime farewell to life; not mourning, but acknowledgement. How
beautiful you are, O life, they say.

One day I wrote a book called *Lemonade Everything was so Infinite*[1] — it
was a book of meditation on one of Kafka's last phrases, a phrase he
wrote down on a sheet of paper, just before his death.

This phrase is 'Limonade es war alles so grenzenlos'.[2]

For me this is *The Poem*, the ecstasy and the regret, the very simple
heart of life.

The ultimate works are short and burning like the fire which reaches
towards the stars. Sometimes they have one line. They are works written

with extraordinary tenderness. Works of gratitude: for life, for death. For it is also as a result of death and *thanks* to death that we discover the splendour of life. It is death that makes us remember the treasures that life contains, with all its living misfortunes and its pleasures.

There is a text which is like a discreet psalm, a song of thanksgiving to death. This text is called *The Hour of the Star*.[3] Clarice Lispector wrote it when she was already almost no one on this earth. The great night was opening forth in all its immensity. A star smaller than a spider was wandering there. This tiny thing, seen at close range, turned out to be a minute human creature, weighing perhaps thirty kilos. But seen from death, or from the stars, she was as big as anything in the world and as important as anyone very important or without importance on our earth.

This minute and almost imponderable person is called Macabea: the book of Macabea is extremely slender, it looks like a very small notebook. It is one of the greatest books in the world.

This book was written by a weary and passionate hand. In a way Clarice had already ceased to be an author, to be a writer. It is the last text, the one which comes *after*. After all books. After time. After the self. It belongs to eternity, to this time of before after me, which nothing can interrupt. To this time, to this secret and infinite life of which we are fragments.

The Hour of the Star tells the story of a minute fragment of human life. Tells faithfully: minutely, fragmentarily.

Macabea is not (only) a character of fiction. She is a speck of dust which got into the author's eye and gave rise to a stream of tears. This book is the stream of tears caused by Macabea. It is also a stream of immense and humble questions which do not ask for answers: they ask for life. This book asks itself: what is an author? Who is worthy of being Macabea's author?

This 'book' murmurs to us: do not the beings who live in a work have a right to the author *they need*?

Macabea needs a very special author. Clarice Lispector creates the necessary author out of love for Macabea.

The Hour of the Star, Clarice Lispector's last hour, is a small, great book which loves and knows nothing, not even its name. I mean not even its title. There are thirteen or fourteen titles. How to choose *one* title? In Macabea's world, choosing is a privilege reserved for the rich. Choosing is martyrdom for the creature who has never had anything. And who thus wants nothing, and wants everything.

So *The Hour of the Star* hesitates. One title is worth another. *The Hour of the Star* is also called: *The Blame is Mine* — or *The Hour of the Star* — or *Let Her Fend for Herself* — or *The Right to Protest* — or *Clarice Lispector* — or. *As for the Future.* — or *Singing the Blues* — or *She Doesn't Know How to Protest* — or *A Sense of Loss* — or *Whistling in the Dark Wind* — or *I Can Do*

Nothing — or *A Record of Preceding Events* — or *A Tearful Tale* — or *A Discreet Exit by the Back Door*.[4]

One creature is worth another.

Another? The other! Ah, the other, that is the name of the mystery, the name of You, the desired one for whom Clarice Lispector has written — all of these books. The other to love. The other who puts love to the test: how to love the other, the strange, the unknown, the not-me-at-all? The criminal, the bourgeoise, the rat, the cockroach — ? How can a woman love a man? or another woman?

The Hour of the Star vibrates wholly with these mysteries.

What follows is a modest meditation on this book which has emerged from the multitude of books to make its way into our hearts tottering like a child.

Now I am going to change tone, to speak a little more coolly about this divine spark.

So *The Hour of the Star* is the story of a person who barely weighs thirty kilos, an inhabitant of *hardly* (in Brazilian, *apenas*), a native of *almost*. What Clarice has done here is to go out to meet the subject who, for her, was the most other possible. Let us try to imagine what would be for each one of us, male and female, the most other possible, the strangest creature possible, while nevertheless remaining within the sphere of the recognizable (I am not talking about Martians, they do not interest me), what is the terrestrial creature that would be *the strangest possible and which would at the same time 'touch' us*. Everyone has their personal stranger. For Clarice it was this little bit of life, coming from the Nordeste. The Nordeste has sadly become famous: people are happy there when they eat rat, it is a land where in our own time people die of starvation in the West. This person comes from the most disinherited place in the world, and the question for Clarice was to work on what it is to be disinherited, to be without inheritance, to the point of being without everything, without memory — though not amnesic — to be so poor that poverty runs through the whole being: the blood is poor, the language is poor, memory is poor; though to be born and to be poor is not a reduction, it is as if one belonged to another planet, a planet from which there is no means of transport to the planet of culture, food, satisfaction, etc.

The 'person'[5] Clarice chose, this almost-a-woman, is a woman who is scarcely a woman, but who is so completely scarcely-a-woman that she is perhaps more of a woman than any woman. She is so small, so minute, that she is right down at the grassroots level of being, and so it is as if she has an almost intimate relationship with the first stirrings of life on earth; she is moreover a blade of grass, and she ends up in the grass, as grass. As a blade of grass, as a slip of a woman, she is situated physically, emotionally, right at the base of genesis, at the beginning and at the end. And so more than we, who are white and heavy, she bears, she displays, the subtlest elements of what we could call 'being-a-woman', because, like extremely poor people, she is attentive and makes us attentive to the insignificances which are our essential riches, and which we, with our ordinary riches, have forgotten and repressed. When she discovers a desire or an appetite, or when she tastes for the first time in her life a food which for us has become the least tempting, the most ordinary of dishes, for her it is a wonder, a most extraordinary discovery. And her wonder gives us back the lost delicacies.

In order to speak in the most intimate way possible about this woman that she is not, that we are not, that I am not, and whom, as Clarice tells us at one point, she must have met by chance in the street on her way to market, it was necessary for Clarice to undergo a superhuman exercise of transferal of all her being, of transformation, of self-estrangement, in order to try to approach such a minute and transparent being. And what did she do to become sufficiently self-estranged? What she did was to be the most other possible from herself, which gave rise to something absolutely remarkable: for the thing the most other possible, was to go into the masculine, *to pass by way of a man*. It is a paradoxical step. Thus in order to approach this almost-a-woman, we see in the text how Clarice has not shaved for several days, has not played football, etc. She goes into the masculine, and this particular masculinity impoverishes her. To go into the masculine is, she suggests, an impoverishment, and like every process of impoverishment with Clarice Lispector, it is a positive movement, a form of asceticism, presented in a thoroughly legible way, a way of bridling a part of pleasure. Moreover in his turn this man 'monasterizes' himself, deprives himself, bows down. Clarice herself gives explanations for this which would doubtless make certain feminists want to burn her on the spot. She says at one point, no one can talk about my heroine, only a man like me can talk about her, because if 'it was a woman writer', she 'would weep soft tears'. This is full of humour, but it forces us to ask questions. We say to ourselves, perhaps it is true that, paradoxically, it is through becoming, through transforming oneself into an author with a beard (he has his own personality, he is not the triumphant author of the mass media, but someone who has come to the end of his life, who says that there is nothing else left for him except writing), it is as a man in extremity, as a being stripped bare, who has given up all pleasures, including football, that Clarice finds the most respectful distance from her little slip of a woman.

We ask ourselves: why would this not have been possible as a woman?

I will answer in Clarice's place, though I only allow myself to do so after long meditation. A woman would perhaps have felt pity, have 'wept soft tears' (this is a wonderful period touch). And pity is not respect. For

Clarice, the supreme value is pitilessness, but a pitilessness full of respect. In the first few pages, she says she has the right to be pitiless. Pity is deforming, it is paternalist, or a kind of mothering, it coats over, covers up, and what Clarice wants to do here is to leave this being naked in her minuscule grandeur.

But — I am going one step further — I am cheating like Clarice in saying what I am saying: yes, a man who does not shave, who is at the end of life, for whom only writing remains, who has no worldly ambition, who only has love — we need to find this man — could be certain of this pitiless attitude. Only this man is Clarice, and yet — this is her genius — she tells us so: the text opens with this famous dedication:

> Dedication of the author
> (in truth Clarice Lispector)

Following which the dedication starts off under the sign of music.

> And so I dedicate this thing to old Shumann and to his sweet Clara, who today are bones, poor us . . . I dedicate myself to the tempest of Beethoven. To the vibration of the neutral colours of Bach. To Chopin who softens my bones. To Stravinski who astonished me and with whom I flew in fire. To 'Death and Transfiguration' where Richard Strauss reveals to me a destiny? Above all, I dedicate myself to the eves of today and to today, to the transparent veil of Debussy, to Marlos Nobre, to Prokofiev, to Carl Orff and Schoenberg . . .[6]

Here we have all the signs and warnings: 'the author (in truth Clarice Lispector)'. This text has as its author a person who discreetly presents herself in the third person between quotation marks — for the author is not simple — moreover there is no real author, there is only an author suspended between '   '. As for Clarice Lispector, she is the truth of this author, but like every truth she is both secret and unknowable. We only know that she is there, like the heart in the breast, we hear her beating the measure of life and she is called 'truth Clarice Lispector'. The truth of Clarice Lispector. (Moreover within this parenthesis another parenthesis opens, into which gnomes, sylphids, dreams, horses, creatures of diverse species, precipitate themselves.)

What she is telling us here is one of the great mysteries of our existence, and this particular mystery is always well hidden in real life, seeing that we are all distributed as men or women on life's stage, and that we take ourselves for men or women. Then, further on in this text, 'naming' herself, Clarice says, only I, 'Rodrigo S.M.', can come to love this girl. As for 'the girl', she takes a name very late in the text in which she arrives like a blade of grass, very slowly. I, 'Rodrigo S.M.', I am in truth Clarice Lispector, put in parentheses, and only the author '(in truth

Clarice Lispector)' can approach this beginning of a woman. This is the impossible truth, *the inexpressible, undemonstrable truth*, which can only be said in parentheses, with several layers of beings working on one another; the impossible truth which cannot be justified before a philosophic tribunal, which cannot pass the bar of monological discourse, or mass-mediatized imaginations. It is the truth which beats like a heart, in the parenthesis of life. And this is our problem: either you understand it, or you do not. Either, or: there are two universes, and these two universes do not communicate. Either you feel it, or you do not. As Clarice says at the end of her dedication, and as she very often says, 'One cannot give proof of the existence of that which is truer, the thing is to believe. *To believe weeping*.'[7] Either we believe weeping, and then we can inhabit the world where the feminine being and the masculine being come into contact, exchange with each other, caress each other, respect each other, are quite incapable of maintaining a discourse as to their exact differences, but live them, these differences, and where — as the opening to the text tells us — if masculine and feminine agree with each other (I cannot say understand each other, because they do not understand each other) it is because there is feminine, there is masculine, in the one and in the other. There are obviously points of conjunction — which does not mean identification.

It was in order to evoke the same mystery that I worked on Rossini's *Tancredi*. What interested me in Rossini's *Tancredi*, and in all the descendants of Tancredi, was the undeveloped mystery, which is not presented with proofs, but which gives itself to be understood weeping, of the existence of a character all the more a man as he is more woman, as she is more man as he is more woman . . . It is easier to do in music than in writing, because music is not subject as the text is to those fearful imperatives of language, which force us to construct sentences with grammatical correctness, attributing genders properly; those who write are called to account. It must be said that it is in poetic writing that something of the mystery and continuity of life can appear, through grammatical subversion, through a certain liberty taken inside language, with regard to the law of gender.

In the course of our research we talk in terms of libidinal economies out of convenience. In order to try to distinguish vital functions, we distinguish two principal libidinal economies; but they do not distinguish themselves in such a decisive way in reality: in the living there are traits which obliterate themselves, which blend together. None the less at the outset one can distinguish structures — I am not saying anything new in this — which we find at work in different societies. We have worked on these economies where it seemed to me to be easiest, most amusing to work on them, approaching them where they are most visible: at the point of what I have called *libidinal education*. We have worked on a group

of texts which belong to what can be called the literature of apprenticeship, the *Bildungsromans*, and all of the texts — and there are a lot of them
because literature is after all their domain — which relate the development of an individual, their story, the story of their soul, the story of their
discovery of the world, of its joys and its prohibitions, its joys and its
laws, always on the trail of the first story of all human stories, the story of
Eve and the Apple. World literature abounds in texts of libidinal
education, because every writer, every artist, is brought at one moment
or another to work on the genesis of his/her own artistic being. It is the
supreme text, the one written through a turning back to the place where
one plays to win or lose life. The stakes are extremely simple, it is a
question of the apple: does one eat it or not? Will one enter into contact
with the intimate inside of the fruit or not?

I have done a lot of work on *primitive scenes*.[8] Will the delightful
Perceval of the *Quest for the Holy Grail* enjoy his marvellous meal or not?
In any case, what is at stake for me in these stories is the fate of the *so-
called 'feminine' economy*; I say 'feminine' economy in connection with
Perceval too, for I do not attribute it to women as an endowment; one
can find these two economies in no matter which individual. *Why
'feminine'*? It is the old story; because in spite of everything, ever since the
Bible and ever since bibles, we have been distributed as descendants of
Eve and descendants of Adam. It is the Book which has written this story.
The Book wrote that the person who had to deal with the question of
pleasure was a woman, was woman; probably because it was indeed a
woman who, in the system which has always been cultural, underwent
this test, which men and women have been subjected to ever since. Every
entry to life finds itself *before the Apple*. What I call 'feminine' and
'masculine' is the relationship to pleasure, the relationship to spending,
because we are born into language, and I cannot do otherwise than to
find myself before words; we cannot get rid of them, they are there. We
could change them, we could put signs in their place, but they would
become just as closed, just as immobile and petrifying as the words
'masculine' and 'feminine' and would lay down the law to us. So there is
nothing to be done, except to shake them like apple trees, all the time.

'An economy said to be F.', 'an economy said to be M.' — why
distinguish between them? Why keep words which are so entirely
treacherous, fearful and war-mongering? This is where all the traps are
set. I give myself a poet's right, otherwise I would not dare to speak. The
right of poets is to say something and then to say, believe it if you want
to, but believe it weeping; or else to erase it, as Genet does, by saying that
all truths are false, that only false truths are true, etc.

In order to define the zones of libidinal, emotional behaviour, where
these structural propensities exert themselves, let us take *the scene of the
apple*.[9] This scene has always struck me because all its elements, which

have become illegible as they have become so familiar to us, are interesting. The first fable of our first book is a fable in which what is at stake is the relationship to the law. There are two principal elements, two main puppets: the word of the Law or the discourse of God and the Apple. It's a struggle between the Apple and the discourse of God. All this transpires in this short scene before a woman. The Book begins *Before the Apple*: at the beginning of everything there is an apple, and this apple, when it is talked about, is said to be a not-to-be-fruit. There is an apple, and straight away there is the law. It is the start of libidinal education, it is here that one begins to share in the experience of the *secret*, because the law is incomprehensible. God says, if you taste the fruit of the tree of knowledge, you will die. It is absolutely incomprehensible. What rich terrain for the theologians and the philosophers, since for Eve 'you will die' does not mean anything, since she is in the paradisiac state where there is no death. She receives the most hermetic discourse there is, the absolute discourse. We will find it again in the story of Abraham who receives an order from God which might also seem incomprehensible, except that Abraham obeys without questioning, absolutely. It is the experience of the secret, the enigma of the apple, of this apple which is invested with every kind of power. And what we are told is that knowledge might begin with the mouth, with the discovery of the taste of something: knowledge and taste go together. What is at stake here is the mystery which is assailed by the law, the law which is absolute, verbal, invisible, negative, it is a symbolic *coup de force* and its force is its invisibility, its non–existence, its force of denial, its 'not'. And facing the law, there is the apple which is, is, is. It is the struggle between presence and absence, between an undesirable, unverifiable, indecisive absence, and a presence, a presence which is not only a presence: the apple is visible and it can be held up to the mouth, it is full, it has an *inside*. And what Eve will discover in her relationship to simple reality, is the inside of the apple, and that this inside is good. This story tells us that the genesis of woman goes through the mouth, through a certain oral pleasure, and through a non-fear of the inside.

If you take Kakfa's famous fable 'Before the Law'[10] the little man from the country, who is partly 'feminine', does not go inside. What is more we do not know if there is an inside. In any case there is a prohibition against the inside which is absolute. In a way there is no inside, since the man who remains before the law, is in fact inside the law. Thus before and inside are the same.

In an astonishing way, our most ancient book of dreams tells us after its own fashion — though we can read it in our own way — that Eve is not afraid of the inside, neither her own, nor that of the other. I would claim that the relationship to the inside, to penetration, to touching the inside is positive. Obviously Eve is punished for it, but that is another matter, that is society's affair. Of course she is punished since she has access to pleasure, of course a positive relationship to the inside is something which threatens society and which must be controlled. That is where the series of 'you-shall-not-enter' begins. It is not insignificant that in the beginning there should be a scene of pleasure which takes this form. It is a game and it is not a game. We find it throughout mythology, throughout literature.

And I find it with Perceval in the *Quest for the Holy Grail*. This is why it is interesting to read the texts which give voice to an unconscious that is completely indifferent to laws, even if the law always catches up with the wild unconscious. To begin with, Perceval is a woman's son, he does not have a father, he is a boy left to his wild state, he is on the side of pleasure, of happiness. Then he is educated and, after a series of trials, he becomes a knight, is covered with armour, becomes phallicized, takes up a sword. One of the major, decisive scenes in the whole story of Perceval is once again the story of Eve and the apple. Perceval, a woman's son, arrives at the court of the Fisher King, a king who is deprived of the use of his legs, a king who is very hospitable and castrated. Perceval is invited to a sumptuous meal during which he takes pleasure in all the excellent foods which are served. Meanwhile there is a procession of servants carrying splendid dishes into another room. Perceval is fascinated by this merry-go-round, he is dying to ask what is going on. But only a short time before, his educator has told him: you are wild, you do not have any manners, but you must learn that in life one-does-not-ask-questions. And Perceval continues to see a lance passing by, and at the end of the lance blood dripping. And while this is happening the narrative intervenes: 'Well, Perceval, are you going to ask questions? You are committing a terrible sin, and you will be punished.' The agonized reader is caught between the narrative and the hero. And Perceval does not ask a single question. The meal ends, the castle disappears in a flash like in a fairy tale, and Perceval meets a maiden who tells him — up until then he did not have a name — 'Now you are called Perceval'. Perceval has committed a dreadful sin, he should have asked who was being served in this way, and since he did not ask, he is punished; he is condemned for the crime (what crime?) he has committed, the immediate consequences of which are catastrophic. He could have saved the Fisher King, the narrative tells us, he could have saved the universe, but the chance has gone. While reading this text I was seized with rage, telling myself it is not fair. I do not see why, nor does Perceval see why, he is punished because he has not done something. And we realize that we are completely in the world of the law which does not have a name or a face, which has the strange property of being entirely negative. It is as if the text were telling you that you are condemned to be inside the law, and that you cannot do otherwise. And at the same time, since the text is a poetic text, it takes into account the world of innocence and the world of pleasure. While the law weaves its web, Perceval is extremely happy, he eats extraordinary things, enjoys himself as much as he can. And suddenly he falls, no, he has fallen into the other world, the world of absolute law which does not give its reasons. By definition undefinable, that is what the law is: pure anti-pleasure. What made Perceval fall in this way is the fact that he is a mother's son, he was brought up in the forest, he is still full of woman's milk. Until he is so violently 'circumcised' that henceforth he takes care of his manly parts.

The relationship to pleasure and the law, the individual's response to this strange, antagonistic relationship indicates whether, we are men or women, different paths through life. It is not anatomical sex that determines anything here. It is, on the contrary, history from which one never escapes, individual and collective history, the cultural schema and the way the individual negotiates with these schema, with these data, adapts to them and reproduces them, or else gets round them, overcomes them, goes beyond them, gets through them — there are a thousand formulae — and joins up with or never joins up with a universe which I would call 'without fear or reproach'. It happens that culturally, women have more of a chance of gaining access to pleasure, because of the cultural and political division of the sexes, which is based on sexual difference, on the way society has used the body and on the fact that it is much easier to inflict on men than on women the horror of the inside. After all women do all virtually or in fact have an experience of the inside, an experience of the capacity for other, an experience of non-negative change brought about by the other, of positive receptivity.

If we resign ourselves to keeping words like 'feminine' and 'masculine' it is because there is an anchoring point somewhere in a far distant reality. But I believe we must do our utmost to reduce this heritage. Let us try as quickly as possible to abandon these binary distinctions which never make any sense.

What can we assign as descriptive traits to these economies? Let us consider our behaviour in life with others, in all the major experiences we encounter, which are the experiences of separation; the experiences, in love, of possession, of dispossession, of incorporation, and non-incorporation, the experiences of mourning, of real mourning, all the experiences which are governed by variable behaviours, economies, structures. How do we lose? How do we keep? Do we remember? Do we forget?

The greatest respect I have for any work whatsoever in the world is the respect I have for the work of Clarice Lispector. She has treated as has no one else to my knowledge all the possible positions of a subject in relation to what would be 'appropriation', use and abuse of owning. And she has done this in the finest and most delicate detail. What her texts struggle against constantly and on every terrain, is the movement of appropriation: for even when it seems most innocent it is still totally destructive. Pity is destructive; badly thought out love is destructive; ill-measured understanding is annihilating. One might say that the work of Clarice Lispector is an immense *book of respect*, a *book of the right distance*. And, as she tells us all the time, one can only attain this right distance through a relentless process of de-selfing, a relentless practice of de-egoization. The enemy as far as she is concerned is the blind self. In *The Hour of the Star* she says, for example,

> The action of this story will result in my transfiguration into others and in my materialization at last into an object. Yes, and perhaps I might reach the sweet flute where I entwine myself in soft liana.[11]

We might say it is only a metaphor; but it is the dream of every author to arrive at such a transfiguration, at such a distancing as to become liana. It is a way of remembering that my self is only one of the elements of the immense mass of material, and only one of the elements haunted by the imaginary.

Another absolutely admirable moment:

> How I should love to hear the pealing of bells in order to work up some enthusiasm as I decipher reality: to see angels flutter like transparent wasps around my fevered head, this head that longs to be ultimately transformed into an object-thing, because so much more simple.[12]

There is also the constant reminder of what we know in the form of a cliché: that we are dust. That we are atoms. And if we did not forget that we were atoms, we would live and we would love differently. More humbly, more expansively. Loving the 'you ares' of the world, as equals. Without design.

Dedication of the author
(in truth Clarice Lispector)

> And so I dedicate this thing to old Schumann and to his sweet Clara, who today are bones, poor us. I dedicate myself to the colour red, bright scarlet, like my blood of a fully-aged man, and so I dedicate myself to my blood. I dedicate myself above all to the gnomes, dwarfs, sylphids, nymphs that inhabit my life. I dedicate myself to the nostalgia for my old poverty, when everything was more sober and dignified and I had never eaten lobster.

What immediately comes through like a burst of lightning in this dedication, apart from the fact that 'the truth' is in between parentheses Clarice Lispector, is the 'I dedicate *myself*'. There is first of all 'I dedicate *this thing* to old Schumann'. We tell ourselves that this must be the book. But the following sentence dedicates 'myself': I *dedicate myself to the colour red of my blood*. In other words, 'this thing' which is the book is 'myself'. This is already the path of metamorphosis: 'I dedicate myself above all to the gnomes, dwarfs, sylphids, nymphs that inhabit my life'. We do not need anything other than this page to replace all the discourses I could produce, that all the analytical texts could produce on the composition of the subject and the question of gender.

> This I who is you, for I can't bear to be simply me, I need the others to hold me up, giddy and awkward as I am, for after all what is there to do except meditate in order to fall into this full emptiness that can only be attained through meditation. Meditating doesn't need to have results. Meditation can have simply itself as an end. I meditate without words and on nothingness. What muddles my life is writing.
>
> And — and not forgetting that though the structure of the atom is invisible, we nevertheless know about it. I know a lot of things that I have never seen. And you do too. One cannot give proof of the existence of that which is truer, the thing is to believe. To believe weeping.[13]

I read this and I tell myself how terrible it is that we spend precious months of our existence trying to give 'proofs', falling into the trap of critical interpellation, allowing ourselves to be led before the tribunal where we are told: give us proof, explain to us what feminine writing or sexual difference is. And if we were more courageous than I am, we would say: a flute for your proof, I am alive. I am not serene enough, except when I write. And when I write I tell myself that it is not enough, we need to do something else. However, it is true that the truest is like this: either you *know* without knowing, and this knowledge which does not know is a flash of joy which the other shares with you, or else there is nothing. We will never convert someone who is not already converted. We will never touch the heart that lives on another planet. I would no longer continue with my seminar if I knew that a sufficiently wide world was reading Clarice Lispector. A few years ago when her texts began to circulate here, I said to myself, I am no longer going to give a seminar, all that is left to do is to read her, everything is said, it is perfect. But as usual everything has been repressed, she has even been transformed in the most extraordinary way, they have embalmed her, had her stuffed as a Brazilian bourgeoise with varnished fingernails. So I carry on my vigil, accompanying her through my reading.

Clarice's texts tell stories in her individual way, they are 'facts', as she says, they are moments, seconds, nows of life, which constantly bring drama into play. Not theatrical tragedies, but the dramas of life. One can include everything that is in convulsion, that seeks to make itself manifest, to accomplish itself. There is a whole series of texts which work on the question of having, *of knowing how to have what one has*. It is one of the most difficult things in the world, since, poor humans that we are, no sooner do we have, than we no longer have. We are often like the fisherman's wife of the tale, who is unhappily prey to the demon of having, of always-having-more: she never has anything of what she has; as soon as she has, she wants the next degree, and so on all the way to infinity, which returns her to zero. To have what we have is the key to happiness. In general we have, we have a great deal, but because we have, we no longer know that we have.

What can we do to have what we have?

We have worked on a marvellous text by Clarice Lispector called 'Clandestine felicity':[14] it is a story about childhood, a magnificent drama just a few pages long. There are two little girls. One is Clarice when she was small. She has a friend whose father is a bookseller, and so she is surely in paradise. But by chance, it is like this in life, the daughter of the bookseller is a little pest. She tells Clarice she is going to lend her an enormous and extraordinary book. She keeps her going for weeks telling her, come to my house, and I will give it to you. Clarice crosses town in a state of absolute happiness, she gets there, the horrid little redhead opens the door, and each time tells her, I have not got it, come back next week, etc. Clarice falls down from the heaven of hope, from hope-heaven. And every time it is the same process of the fall into the abyss and the climb out of the abyss and the extraordinary surge of happiness which starts all over again. Without fail Clarice comes back to the door, until the day when the mother of the horrid little girl appears on the scene, and discovers the mechanism of hate which has been put into operation. The mother is devastated by the discovery of her daughter's wickedness, but, mother of all the little girls in the world, she immediately makes amends. She insists on the book being lent. And furthermore, Clarice adds, the mother says 'You may keep it as long as you want to'. She gives her the infiniteness of this book. But from the moment when Clarice can dispose of this book infinitely, the race across town, the desire, everything which has been tortured happiness is forgotten, since she has everything, and for ever, but with a limit: the book has not been given to her, it has been lent to her for as long as she wants. And this is the moral of the story: it is yours for as long as you have the strength to want it. And Clarice invents the marvellous, magical means, the art of remaining on the brink, to make this 'as long as' interminable. She *has* the book; what must she do to 'have' it? This is where she begins to enjoy what she has and not what she desires, and so she makes the having it palpitate, she begins to bring it into play, to make it stir slightly, to make it vibrate, and through a sort of fabulous intuition, she does not consume it, she does not devour it: she starts by making a sandwich, she comes and goes between the kitchen and the book, the bread sandwich and the textual sandwich which she does not devour, and then she tells us how she sits down in a Brazilian hammock with her book on her knees, which she literally rocks, and does not read, does not read, not yet — and then she goes off again. She has found all of the most profound, the most delicate, the finest ruses, to continue to have what she has eternally. She calls this 'clandestine felicity'. Yes, felicity can only be clandestine, it will always be clandestine, happiness is its own secret, we need to know that we can only have if we know how to have in a way which does not destroy, does not possess, preserves.

The secret is to remember at every moment what a blessing it is to have.

To keep in the having the breathless lightness of hoping to have.

To have just after not having had. To always have in us the emotion of having almost not had. For to have is always a miracle.

And to constantly rediscover in the having the surprise of receiving.

In the texts of Clarice Lispector, we find all the lessons of knowledge, but it is a knowledge of how to live, not a scholarly knowledge. One of the first lessons about living is the one about knowing how to not know, which does not mean not knowing, but *knowing how to not know*, knowing how to avoid getting closed in by knowledge, knowing more and less than what one knows, knowing how to not understand, while never being on the side of ignorance. It is not a question of not having understood anything, but of not letting oneself get locked into comprehension. Each time that we come to know something, in reality it is a step. Then we have to strike out for the un-known, to make our way along in the dark, with an 'apple in our hand' like a candle.[15]

To find the apple by feeling one's way along in the dark, this is the condition of discovery, this is the condition of love. As Clarice says in 'The Foreign Legion'[16] 'Because I do not know how to do anything, because I remember nothing and because it is night, I hold out my hand and I save a child'.[17] So I translate: I can only save a child on two conditions, the one is only the condition of the other: on condition of not preceding the child, on condition of not knowing any more than he or she does; of not having the massive, old heavy memory which would crush the young budding memory of the child. It is only from the dark of my night that I can hold out my hand.

The title story of the *The Foreign Legion* is a pitiless tale that concerns the adult Clarice and a little girl who lives in her building and whose name is Ofelia. This little girl forcefully invites herself into Clarice's apartment, she is already a little woman, she is in the position of absolute mastery, she is imperious, authoritative, and she instructs Clarice: you should not have bought that, you should not have done that; there is a sort of inversion of roles, until the day that the little girl becomes a little girl again under the influence of a gift. One day Ofelia hears a cheeping sound in the kitchen, it is the cheeping of a tiny baby chick. For the first time something precedes her, she is caught off her guard. Clarice sees a terrible drama in Ofelia's eyes: she has been pierced for the first time by the torturing arrow of desire. She struggles as if in a death agony against the pain of this desire, she does not want to enter this wounded world, this world of love, and to be at the mercy of the other. It is with her reluctant body that she discovers how desire can present an opening to the other, a possibility of being hurt, of being changed. Finally she succumbs, she cannot help seeing the desire growing in her, but she does not want to show this to Clarice. Then there is a wonderful scene: Clarice understands everything that is happening, and wonders how she can give the chick to the little girl as she sees she will die if she does not have it. But she cannot give it to her, because the little girl, erect, stiff with refusal, her heart strings taut, would find herself in the position of someone to whom one has given a gift, and who would thus be in debt. All of the simplest, the most elementary, the most terrible mechanisms of gift and debt, of exchange and gratitude are put into operation: Clarice cannot give it to her without the gift being cancelled out. If the little girl has to say thank you, she will not have anything. Thus the only means of giving her the chick is to let her take it: for Clarice, in the position of symbolic mother, to efface herself, to retire in such a way that the child may benefit from the gift as if it were given by God, by no one, and thus be free of all feelings of debt. The little girl finally goes to the kitchen alone. The text notes an immense silence, the little girl comes back, Clarice rushes into the kitchen and finds the chick dead. We understand in this kitchen the drama of gift and debt, our own daily drama, we who are so often victims of the structure of debt. The inevitability of this scene: Clarice will have given the baby chick to the little girl as best she can, no more, no less. And the state of the little girl is such that she can only possess the chick by losing it the moment she has it. The chick is too much for her, and yet she has had it as much but also as little as she could. Clarice let her take it as much as she was able to, and thus to the point of total loss.

In *A Paixão segundo G.H. (The Passion according to G.H.)*, we reach after a long journey this phrase of Clarice's:

Now I need your hand, not for me not to be afraid, but for you not to be afraid. I know that believing in all this will be, in the beginning, your great solitude. But the moment will come when you will give me your hand, no longer out of solitude, but like me now: out of love. Like me, you will not be afraid to mingle in God's extreme energetic gentleness. Solitude is having only the human destiny.

And solitude is not needing.[18]

Listen to it carefully, for this is really the most beautiful, the noblest definition of a certain economy that I allow myself to call 'feminine'.

Not needing leaves a man very alone, all alone. Ah, needing does not isolate the person, the thing needs the thing . . .

Ah, my love, don't be afraid of want: it is our greatest destiny. Love is so much more fatal than I had thought, love is as inherent as want itself, and we are guaranteed by a necessity which will be renewed continuously. Love already is, is always.[19].

What Clarice is establishing here, in this hymn to want, is something which would would greatly surprise many theoreticians of lack, it is the economy of positive lack: above all let us not be lacking in lack.

'Love already is.' It is there. It precedes us as the poem precedes the
And the miracle also is asked for, and is had, for continuity has interstices which do not discontinue it, the miracle is the note which is between the number one and the number two. One only has to need and one has.[20]

All we need to do is to need and we have. All we need to do is to not be afraid of needing and we have. All we need to do is to not do like little Ofelia who was afraid of needing and who with a bound leapt into the scene of castration.

'Love already is.' It is there. It precedes us as the poem precedes the poet. 'All that is lacking is the *coup de grâce* which is called passion.' It is the economy of thankfulness. All we need to do is to live and we have. Another way that Clarice would say this is: hunger is faith.

But Kafka, at the same extremity of life, says this: 'Man kann doch nicht nicht-leben' ('One cannot however not-live'). It is the model of the economy of double impotence. At the end of life, and before death, Kafka and Clarice Lispector ask themselves how to accomplish the truth of our human being.

Clarice is on the side of yes: 'all we need to do is to live and this in itself becomes a great goodness', anyone who accepts living is good, anyone who is thankful for living is good and does good: this is sainthood according to Clarice Lispector. It is a modest kind of sainthood. On the other bank of living Kafka says, 'Dass es uns an Glauben fehle, kann man nicht sagen' ('It cannot be said that we lack faith'). We are in the negative discourse. Everything is there: faith, lack, need, life, but everything is caught up in the not. It is a resignation to, not an exaltation of existence.

Dass es uns an Glauben fehle, kann man nicht sagen. Allein die einfache Tatsache unseres Lebens ist in ihrem Glaubenswert gar nicht auszuschöpfen. (It cannot be said that we lack faith. In itself the simple fact that we live is endowed with a value of faith.)

And then he adds

'Hier wäre ein Glaubenswert?' (Would this be a value of faith?)

And he replies, because he is a divided being:

Man kann doch nicht nicht-leben. Eben in diesem, 'kann doch nicht' steckt die wahnsinnige Kraft des Glaubens; in dieser Verneinung bekommt sie Gestalt. (One cannot however not-live. It is precisely in this 'cannot-however' that the mad force of faith resides; it is in this negation that it takes shape.)[21]

It is the opposite, in the same place of meditation, of Clarice's faith: to come to think that solitude is to not need, that to need is already to break with solitude, is the greatest lesson in humility.

These positions of humility and non-humility carry along with them certain styles, certain kinds of writing.

Not long ago I distinguished between two sorts of styles: one of which I have called (echoing the title of a text by Clarice) *the style of live water*, where thirst is itself that which quenches, since to be thirsty is already to give oneself drink. This style of live water gives rise to works which are like streams of blood or water, which are full of tears, full of drops of blood or tears transformed into stars. Made up of phrases which spill forth dripping, in luminous parataxis.

However, from the same analyses, from the same visions of the world, but lived out differently, we have a style marked by the pain of reduction, a 'man's' style which is at the mercy of scenes of castration. This gives rise to forms which are dry, stripped bare, marked by the negative, forms of which the most striking examples are those of Kafka and Blanchot.

If I come back to 'men' and 'women', it is not my fault. I do sometimes work on forms of economies which are open, expansive, generous, daring, in texts such as those of Kleist, Genet, etc; as for Shakespeare, he always precedes us. There are texts by men who are capable of other. And if we are sent back to sexual identity cards, it is just a cultural curse. The problem is not with men: one finds a great deal of femininity in men, the problem is with the women who have produced, who have written, because culturally, they have been subjected to the obligations of masculinization in order to hoist themselves on to the scene of socio-political legitimation. With the result that most of the texts by women up to our own time have been terribly marked by the 'masculine' economy.

The Economy of Mansuetude

Rare indeed are texts like those of Clarice's: texts which, without denying that we all have to cope with solitude, hold out their hand to us and help us to attain the world of mansuetude. I take the word *mansuetude* literally: it is *the habit of holding out one's hand*. There are two or three essential texts of Clarice's which tell us everything about mansuetude: a text called 'The Partaking of the Breads',[22] which works on blessing, and 'So Much Mansuetude'.[23]

So Much Mansuetude

So the obscure hour, perhaps the most obscure hour, in the middle of the day, preceded this thing that I even do not want to attempt to define. In the middle of the day it was night, and this thing that I do not want to define yet is a tranquil light inside of me, and this they would call serene joy. I am a little disoriented as if a heart had been pulled out of me, and in its place were now a sudden absence, an almost palpable absence of what was before an organ bathed in the obscurity of pain. I am not feeling anything. But this is the opposite of a torpor. It's a lighter and more silent way of existing.

But I am also uneasy. I was organized to console myself from anguish and pain. But how do I handle myself with this simple and tranquil joy. Because I am not used to not needing my own consolation. The word consolation happened without my feeling, and I didn't note it, and when I went to search for it, it had already transformed itself into

Tanta Mansidão

Pois a hora escura, talvez a mais escura, em pleno dia, precedeu essa coisa que não quero sequer tentar definir. Em pleno dia era noite, e essa coisa que não quero ainda definir é uma luz tranqüila dentro de mim, e a ela chamariam de alegria, alegria mansa. Estou um pouco desnorteada como se um coração me tivesse sido tirado, e em lugar dele estivesse agora a súbita ausência, uma ausência quase palpável do que era antes um órgão banhado da escuridão da dor. Não estou sentindo nada. Mas é o contrário de um torpor. É um modo mais level e mais silencioso de existir.

Mas estou também inquieta. Eu estava organizada para me consolar da angústia e da dor. Mas como é que me arrumo com essa simples e tranqüila alegria. É que não estou habituada a não precisar de meu próprio consolo. A palavra consolo aconteceu sem eu sentir, e eu não notei, e quando fui procurá-la, ela já se havia transformado em carne e flesh and spirit, already it didn't exist anymore as a thought.

I go then to the window, it is raining hard. Out of habit I am searching in the rain what in another moment would serve me as a consolation. But I don't have any pain to console.

Ah, I know. I'm now searching in the rain for a joy so great that it becomes sharp, and it puts me in contact with a sharpness that resembles the sharpness of pain. But the search is useless. I am at the window and only this happens: I see with beneficient eyes the rain, and the rain sees me in agreement with me. We're both busy flowing. How long will my state last? I notice that, with this question, I am fingering my pulse to feel where will be the painful throbbing from before. And I see that the throbbing pain is not there.

Scarcely this: it's raining and I'm seeing the rain. What simplicity. I never thought the world and I would arrive at this point of wheat. The rain falls not because she needs me, and I watch the rain not because I need her. But we are as much together as the water of the rain is bound to the rain. And I'm not thanking anything. Hadn't I, just after being born, voluntarily and necessarily taken the path that I took — and I would have always been really what I am being: a countrywoman who is in a field where it is raining. Without

espírito, já não existia mais como pensamento.

Vou então à janela, está chovendo muito. Por hábito estou procuranda na chuva o que em outro momento me serviria de consolo. Mas não tenho dor a consolar.

Ah, eu sei. Estou agora procurando na chuva uma alegria tão grande que se torne aguda, e que me ponha em contato com uma agudez que se pareça a agudez da dor. Mas é inútil a procura. Estou à janela e só acontece isto: vejo com olhos benéficos a chuva, e a chuva me vê de acordo comigo. Estamos ocupadas ambas em fluir. Quanto durará esse meu estado? Percebo que, com esta pergunta, estou apalpando meu pulso para sentir onde estará o latejar dolorido de antes. E vejo que não há o latejar da dor.

Apenas isso: chove e estou vendo a chuva. Que simplicidade. Nunca pensei que o mundo e eu chegássemos a esse ponto de trigo. A chuva cai não porque está precisando de mim, e eu olho a chuva não porque preciso dela. Mas nós estamos tão juntas como a água da chuva está ligada à chuva. E eu não estou agradecendo nada. Não tivesse eu, logo depois de nascer, tomado involuntária e forçadamente o caminho que tomei — e teria sido sempre o que realmente estou sendo: uma camponesa que está num campo onde chove. Nem sequer

even thanking God or nature. The rain thanks nothing either. I am not a thing which gives thanks for having been transformed into another. Am a woman, am a person, am an attention, am a body looking out of the window. Just as the rain is not grateful for not being a stone. She is a rain. Perhaps this is what we can call being alive. No more than this, but this: alive. And simply alive from a serene joy.	agradecendo ao Deus ou à natureza. A chuva também não agradece nada. Não sou uma coisa que agradece ter se transformado em outra. Sou uma mulher, sou uma pessoa, sou uma atenção, sou um corpo olhando pela janela. Assim como a chuva não é grata por não ser uma perdra. Ela é uma chuva. Talvez seja isso ao que se poderia chamar de estar vivo. Não mais que isto, mas isto: vivo. E apenas vivo de uma alegria mansa.

There is the world and the self: everything. 'I go to the window, it's raining hard.' It is the meeting of two equivalents. Not the equivalents of Genet for whom all beings are equivalent to one another by the wound of castration. It is the rain and her. It is the encounter which is called something wonderful: 'this point of wheat'. There where the rain and she encounter each other, there is wheat. And then this affirmation with its implacable justice: 'I am not a thing which gives thanks for having been transformed into another'. No thanks, no pity, no acknowledgement, no debt, but being, being, with insistence — without commentary. A pure 'here I am'.

Am a woman, am a person, am an attention, am a body looking out of the window. Just as the rain is not grateful for not being a stone.

It is the separation of positive and negative. I am she who–not, I am, am, am. Perhaps this is what one could call living. It is not the economy of consolation. I cannot say that everyone can situate themselves there where Clarice situates herself: beyond anguish, beyond mourning, in the magnificent acceptance of being she who simply encounters the rain. One needs to be very strong, and very humble, to be able to say 'I am a woman', continuing of course with 'am a person, am an attention'. It is not 'I am a woman', full stop. But 'am a body looking out of the window'. Whoever can say, 'I am a body looking out of a window', can say 'I am a woman'. Woman is she who 'is' woman *and*, woman making her way forward in the world taking heed.

Heed. Need.

This I Who Is You

Who are you? In numerous texts by Clarice Lispector, the most extreme approach, the greatest tension is situated between the human subject and the non-human subject. The partner, the other, the one with whom it becomes a question of establishing a love relationship, at the end of a very long quest, is the rat in 'Vengeance and Painful Reconciliation'.[24] In the text called 'Mineirinho',[25] the other is a sort of human rat, a delinquent, a bandit, who is killed like a rat, and with whom Clarice has the greatest difficulty in establishing a communicative relationship. It is often the non-human subject which has the strongest effect, the most striking example being the cockroach in *The Passion according to G.H.* This woman, G.H., who does not have a name, of whom only the barest initials remain, goes a long way, all the way to the immemorial cockroach. (This cockroach is the great Brazilian cockroach; in Brazil-ian, it is feminine, *barata*.) She travels a hundred thousand years in a room before coming to the end of this painstaking journey from which not a single step can be omitted otherwise it would all be over, she would have skipped a stage in this step-by-step process where the steps are not the steps of humans, but the steps of a cockroach. It is with insect legs that she advances all the way to the cockroach, and this is where the famous scene takes place, which is immense, and which must not be misunder-stood: the scene of 'tasting the cockroach'. G.H. thinks she is at the point of maturation where she will be able to love, to make way for the other, make the supreme gesture with regard to the cockroach. Having inadvertently trapped the cockroach in the cupboard door, and the cockroach having let out a little of its juice, of its matter — but cockroaches are immortal beings, they have existed for millions of years — she holds some of the cockroach's white matter up to her mouth, and then a violent incident occurs: she disappears, she vomits with disgust, she faints, vomits herself up. And the marvellous thing about this story is that she realizes that she was mistaken: her mistake was that she did not leave room for the other, and that, in the immoderateness of love, she told herself, I am going to dominate my disgust, and I am going to go as far as the gesture of supreme communion, 'I am going to embrace the leper'. It is a mistake. The embrace with the leper transformed into metaphor has lost its truth. G.H. makes the gesture, which she does not analyse at the time, of incorporation. She immediately vomits the cockroach, and the step-by-step, insect-like approach begins again all the way to the ultimate revelation. The most difficult thing to do is to arrive at the most extreme proximity while guarding against the trap of projection, of identification. The other must remain in all its extreme strangeness within the greatest possible proximity. In *The Passion*, the subject with whom Clarice does this work, the love partner, is sufficiently strange for the work to be done in a way that is more obvious to us than if the other were an ordinary human subject.

But Clarice's ultimate project is to make the other human subject appear equal to — and this is positive — the cockroach. All of her repeated endeavours, each one more powerful and more precise than the other, are brought to a peak in *The Hour of the Star*, where Macabea (this is the name that the scarcely-a-woman will bear very late in the text, the name she comes into) is there in place of the cockroach. She is a talking cockroach, and she is as ancient, as primitive as the cockroach.

And all this is done with the assistance of, to the accompaniment of music.

> I dedicate *myself* to the eves of today and to today, to the transparent veil of Debussy, to Marlos Nobre, to Prokofiev, to Carl Orff and Schoenberg, to the dodecaphonists, to the rasping cries of the electronic ones — to all those who in me have reached terribly unhoped-for zones, all of these prophets of the present . . .

It is vital to say 'the prophets of the present', because it is the present we always miss:

> and who have predicted me to myself, to the point that at this moment I explode into: I.[26]

Those who help us to explode into 'I' are perhaps those who, by ways which are not the ways of discourse, but the ways of the voice, reach, awaken in us the 'unhoped-for zones'. Those who are the thieves of fire, the stealers of music.

But in the text, 'the prophets of the present', who are at the same time giants — Debussy, Schoenberg or Prokofiev, the great composers, each of whom touches her, 'the author', at a different point of her body — do not exist for the lowly little characters who are the inhabitants of the book. Once we have entered the poverty of the text through this door, what remains of these great lords of music is what punctuates the text from time to time in a way that is extremely painful for us: there is a violinist, for example, whose sawing we hear interrupted now and then in the text; and there is the whole range of the cry.[27] On the first page we have the most elementary music:

> The toothache that passes through this narrative has given me a sharp twinge right in the mouth. I break out into a strident, high-pitched, syncopated melody. It is the sound of my own pain, of someone who carries this world where there is so little happiness.[28]

I come back to the music. When I spoke about Tancredi, I had been working on the interplay of the categories of the 'faithful' and the 'unfaithful'. In *Jerusalem Delivered* the faithful and the unfaithful constantly exchange themselves, exactly as 'men' and 'women' do in the domain of sexual difference. There are two couples of lovers, one of them is the classical couple, Rinaldo and Armida, in which one sees a banal story of seduction played out between a *femme fatale* and a castrated man. And then there is the other couple, Tancredi and Clorinda, at the opposite pole from Rinaldo and Armida, who remain outside of the scene of seduction, who remain in a state of admiration, a value we do not talk about enough, and which is akin to respect. Tancredi and Clorinda particularly moved me because there is an imaginary universe in literature where one meets 'the armed woman'. It would be easy to treat her as a type, we could say she is the amazon, yes they exist; or she is a fantasy, a historic reality, I do not know, it does not matter. But in the most ancient of epic poems, in the most ancient stories, there are these women who go forth to meet men as equals in the exercise of power and war, and this always turns into love. Perhaps this is an allegory of love. What is most interesting is to see the displacements of the classical allegory all the way to what would be the sign, the announcement, of another type of love relationship. For example, Kleist's play *Penthesilea* portrays a highly complex relationship of reversals where Achilles tries to cross over on to the side of femininity and where Penthesilea has difficulty reconciling the obligation of being a man with the need to be a woman. Clorinda is the best warrior of the infidel army, she's a woman and she's the most faithful of women. What is beautiful about the story of *Jerusalem Delivered*, is that Tancredi pursues Clorinda, equal pursues equal, the strongest pursues the strongest, the most beautiful pursues the most beautiful. Until Clorinda accidentally loses her helmet and Tancredi sees in a dazzling scene that the being who has attracted him across fields and through songs has long hair. And so the drama of Tancredi and Clorinda is set ablaze. Tancredi adores Clorinda, everything separates them. For they are the subjects of the fatality that governs all the great epics. And as happens to Perceval in the *Quest for the Holy Grail*, the law intervenes to say be careful, we are in the world of the law, even if you think otherwise. In these epics, whenever there is the possibility of a happy love between two equal masculine and feminine forces, cultural reality hastily intervenes to forbid it. Thus we can be sure that Tancredi and Clorinda will come to grief, because they love each other as equals, with equal strength, with equal loyalty. History will not tolerate it, one of them has to die. And in this final, terrible, accidental struggle, Tancredi kills Clorinda, because he has not recognized her wearing a different helmet. It is in death that they rejoin each other, because this is how history wants it. But desire wants something else.

I follow Tancredi's footsteps, and I come to the *Tancredi* of Rossini. Here is a story in which the musician has heard the most profound reality with the ear of desire. What he heard was the truth of this love. Rossini has written a work which stages the pursuits, the struggles between Tancredi and Clorinda. (Clorinda has changed her name and is called Amenaïde, but that does not alter the desire.) Without any explanation, in accordance with the marvellous right of all musicians, a right which I envy, Tancredi is a woman, is sung by a woman and no one in the theatre thinks of asking for an account of the necessary displacement Rossini has imposed. It is in the world of music that a certain strength full of gentleness is assigned, without any ulterior motives and without any premeditation, to a woman's voice. Rossini's Tancredi doesn't turn round and ask am I a man or a woman? It is true that Clorinda (or Amenaïde) can only be loved by a Tancreda.[29] When we read *Jerusalem Delivered*, there is a man and a woman who wear armour. But how is this armour to be got rid of? Then we hear the (feminine) Tancreda of Rossini and these questions no longer exist. In essence they are two women. Still one of them is also a man, but a man in so far as she is capable of woman, capable of Amenaïde. These are mysteries that we live in our daily lives, which are forbidden, because they are unclassifiable in the social imaginary. And yet they are what life is all about.

In *The Hour of the Star* there is a metamorphosis, and a metamorphosis which is to be accomplished not by the desire of metamorphosis, but by the movement of recognition of the other. And this movement is perhaps best expressed in a confidence which 'the author (in truth Clarice Lispector)' makes when he (she) says: it's the highest point of the inscription of the virtuality of the other: 'When I consider that I might have been born her —'. The author is talking about Macabea who does not yet have a name:

> She indulged in certain little pleasures. On wintry nights, shivering from head to foot under a thin cotton sheet, she would read by candle-light the advertisements that she had cut out of old newspapers lying around the office. She collected newspaper advertisements, and pasted them into an album.[30]

These are pleasures that we no longer have. We are people living after lobster. But before lobster, one has the greatest pleasures in the world. For example, this vast world of the 'little ads', the world of promises. By collecting advertisements, she brings about the recreation of the promised land.

> The advertisement she treasured most of all was in colour: it advertised a face cream for women with complexions so very different from her own sallow skin. Blinking furiously (a fatal tic that she had recently acquired), she imagined the pleasure of possessing such luxuries. The cream looked so appetizing that, were she to find enough money to buy it, she wouldn't be foolish.

Never mind her skin! She would eat the cream, she would, in large spoonfuls straight from the jar. She was needing to put on some flesh, for her body was drier than a half-empty sack of toasted breadcrumbs. With time, she had become transformed into mere living matter in its primary state. Perhaps this was her protection from the enormous temptation to be unhappy and to feel sorry for herself. (When I consider that I might have been born her — and why not? — I shudder. The fact that I am not her strikes me as being a cowardly escape. I feel remorse, as I explained in one of my titles for this book.)[31]

'The advertisement she most treasures' is the one that questions all the poverty of feminity, as well as all the possible richness of femininity. In this paragraph, we circulate between: I am not, I could be her, as we advance along the most powerful path of meditation that we can possibly pursue while thinking of the other. In general, when we think of the other, it is in terms of negative non–identification, of exclusion, whereas here there is a recognition of the difference of the other, but accompanied by the continual raising of the possibility of being the other. Thus simply, 'these women's complexions were not hers', and if she had the jar — what a marvellous thing — she would do with it what those who live after lobster would never think of doing. She would eat it. For she is at the most rudimentary level of cream; at the most elementary level of food. And it is true that she is made of 'crumbs'. She has ovaries which are 'dry little mushrooms'. That is how she sees herself. 'The temptation to be unhappy and to feel sorry for herself' would deprive her of the joy of being alive. Because Macabea, in her infinite poverty, preserves the 'it's enough to live' of *The Passion according to G.H.* What she has is simply living. Not the eating and drinking, which she is almost without. This poverty is her richness. It is what we do not have, we who have lost the paradise of before–lobster. '(When I consider that I might have been born her —)', it is the author who says this, in the masculine, it is his parenthesis. This 'I who is you', and who thus could be her, but who happily and unhappily is not her. (It is the opposite of the parenthesis of the Dedication which says 'Dedication of the author (in truth Clarice Lispector)'. Here in the parenthesis, '(When I consider that I might have been born her — and why not? — I shudder (. . .))', is the climax of the development proposed in '(in truth Clarice Lispector)'. All the chances are in the parentheses, it is the chance of birth, it is the moment when matter precipitates itself into form, and which results in a Macabea or an author or a Clarice or us. This chance is in the parenthesis. 'Why not?' — this is Clarice's ethical question. I was born Clarice, but by chance. We know that she was born in the Ukraine and that she writes in Brazilian. She is moreover the greatest Brazilian writer, but she could just as well have been a pygmy, and why not? We always identify with our chances, our accidents, we the superior beings of after-the-lobster.

But this identification is narcissistic and impoverishing. We are much more than what our own name authorizes us to believe we are.

We are *possible*. We only need to avoid closing up the parentheses in which our 'why-nots' live. Thus I am a person who begins a long time before me, with the first molecules, and who continues after me and all around me. However and by chance I am a woman, and I belong to the human race. Ah yes, I am human and what is more, a woman.

And at the same time it is the confession of terror, what if I the author, 'Rodrigo S.M.', had been born Macabea. '(The fact that I am not her strikes me as being a cowardly escape. I feel remorse, as I explained in one of my titles).' The text will have been an immense endeavour to have known at least one life of Macabea. When Clarice goes by way of Macabea, after a series of metamorphoses, when she returns to matter, reappears as a masculine author, etc, it is the moment in which she will soon in reality cease to be a person called Clarice Lispector. The moment of this metamorphosis is so brief — *The Hour of the Star* is a very short book — you can read it in an hour — and this story of the life of Clarice Lispector is the last. It is perhaps in effect in her last hour that 'the author (in truth Clarice Lispector)' will have succeeded in being born Macabea, Macabea, the name of Clarice Lispector become no one, and whose live elements are there, invisible, in the air we breathe.

The author of *The Hour of the Star* is a woman of such delicacy. The author of the author of *The Hour of the Star* is born out of the necessity of this text, and he dies with the text. He is the work of his work. He is the child, the father and (in truth the mother).

He has been brought into the world with the mission to love in the best way possible the scarcely-a-woman Macabea. To love her entirely and in detail, she whom no one other than No one has known how to love.

And with the mission to love her sparse hair and her sex of nevertheless-a-woman. This is the delicate task that Clarice Lispector has confided to the author whom she has created expressly for Macabea, for perhaps a woman (in truth Clarice Lispector) would not have dared to contemplate a woman's sex.

And perhaps the modest Macabea would have been much more frightened by a woman's gaze than by that of a man. Thus Clarice withdraws out of love, and delegates Rodrigo S.M. to Macabea's side.

And is it not just that the characters should have a right to the author who is *best placed* to understand them and give them life?

Obviously this remark only holds true for books where it is a question *of loving*, of respecting.

And the respect must begin *before* the book.

How far it is from a star to a self, O what inconceivable proximity between one species and another, between an adult and a child, between an author and a character what an unfathomable distance, from one heart to another what secret proximity.

Everything is far away, not everything resides only in distance, everything is less distant than we think, in the end everything touches, touches us.

As Macabea got into Clarice's eye, like a speck of dust, as she made her weep tears of believing.

I am touched by Clarice's voice.

The step of her slow, heavy phrases weighs on my heart, she treads with short heavy phrases, thoughtfully.

Sometimes one has to go very far.
Sometimes the right distance is extreme remoteness.
Sometimes it is in extreme proximity that it breathes.

Notes

1. *Limonade tout était si infini*, Paris, Editions des femmes, 1982. The English translation *Lemonade Everything was so Infinite* by Ann Liddle is pending publication with Editions des femmes.
2. Kafka's phrase can be found in the published correspondence *Briefe 1902–1924*, in the section entitled 'Aus den Gespräch Blättern', New York, Schocken Books, 1958, p. 491.
3. *A Hora da Estrela*, Rio de Janeiro, Livraria José Olimpio Editora, 1979, (5th edition). Translated into English as *The Hour of the Star*, by Giovanni Pontiero, Manchester, Carcanet, 1986. All subsequent page references are to the English translation.
4. Giovanni Pontiero's translation.
5. The word *personne* in French means both 'person' and 'no one'.
6. All quotations from the author's dedication to *The Hour of the Star* are translated here by Sarah Cornell and Ann Liddle.
7. Added emphasis.
8. In the French this is written as 'les s-cènes primitives' with a play on the word *scène* (scene) and its homophone *cène* (from the Latin *cena* — evening meal). *La cène* is also the French expression for 'The Last Supper'.
9. The play on words is repeated in the French here as *'la s-cène de la pomme'* (see note 8).
10. The reference here is to the story which Kafka wrote in 1914 as part of *The Trial*, English edition translated by Edwin and Willa Muir, New York, Schocken Books, 1977, pp. 213–15 (15th printing). The story also appears in

The Complete Stories, New York, Schocken Books, 1971. (The story concerns a man from the country who tries to gain admittance to the law.

11. Translated here by Sarah Cornell and Marguerite Sandré, the passage appears on page 20 of the Carcanet edition.
12. Giovanni Pontiero's translation, p. 17.
13. From the author's Dedication to The Hour of the Star.
14. In Felicidade Clandestina, Rio de Janeiro, Nova Fronteira, 1971.
15. The Apple in the Dark is the title of a book by Clarice Lispector. The Brazilian reference is A Maçã no Escuro, São Poulo, Circulo do Livro, 1961. The English translation is by Gregory Rabassa, London, Virago, 1985.
16. 'The Foreign Legion', in The Foreign Legion, translated by Giovanni Pontiero, Carcanet, Manchester, 1986, pp. 87–101. The Brazilian reference is 'A Legião Estrangeira' in A Legião Estrangeira, São Paulo, Ática, 1982.
17. Translated by Sarah Cornell and Ann Liddle, A Legião Estrangera, p. 101.
18. A Paixão segundo G.H., Rio de Janeiro, Editora do Autor, 1964. This quote, which is from pp. 171–2 of the Brazilian, is translated by Mairéad Hanrahan.
19. From A Paixão segundo G.H., p. 172, translated by Mairéad Hanrahan.
20. From A Paixão segundo G.H., p. 171, translated by Mairéad Hanrahan.
21. The quotation is from Kafka's '4th Octavo Notebook' (fragment written in 1918), in Hochzeitsvor bereitungen auf dem Lande (Wedding Preparations in the Country), Frankfurt, T.B. Fischer, 1980, p. 91.
22. Translated as 'The Sharing of Bread' in The Foreign Legion, Giovanni Pontiero, Carcanet, 1986, pp. 28–30. The Brazilian reference is 'A Repartição dos Pães', in Felicidade Clandestina, Rio de Janeiro, Editora Nova Fronteira, 1971.
23. 'Tanta Mansidão' ('So Much Mansuetude'), in Onde Estivetes de Noite, Rio de Janeiro, Editora Nova Fronteira, 1974, pp. 115–19. This translation is by Sarah Cornell, Catherine Franke, Camillo Penna and Ann Liddle.
24. In The Foreign Legion, translated by Giovanni Pontiero, Carcanet, 1986, pp. 193–6. The Brazilian reference is 'A Vingança e a Reconcilia çao Penosa', in Para Não Esquecer, São Paulo, Editora Ática, 1979.
25. In The Foreign Legion, translated by Giovanni Pontiero, Carcanet, pp. 212–15. The Brazilian reference is in Para Não Esquecer (see note 24).
26. From the author's Dedication to The Hour of the Star.
27. The phrase echoes one of the titles of The Hour of the Star.
28. Giovanni Pontiero's translation, p. 12.
29. The feminine is emphasized in the French through the underlined use of the indefinite article 'une'.
30. Giovanni Pontiero's translation, p. 38.
31. Giovanni Pontiero's translation, p. 38.

3

Tancredi continues

Hélène Cixous

Translated from the French by Ann Liddle
and Susan Sellers

I read *Jerusalem Delivered*, rushing headlong into the fray, merging with other impetuous bodies, troubled bodies, delimited bodies.

Two camps dispute the body of the Beloved. I mean Jerusalem. Two camps, always the same. Today as at the time of the Crusades as in Paradise.

But it is not the story of the war between the Faithful and the Unfaithful that interests me, it is the other story, the one hidden by history, the one of two beings, two others who cannot remain prisoners in their camps, do not want to win the war, but want to win life or to lose it. What holds me is the story of love, in other words the story of the other and its other. Not Rinaldo and Armida, Same-Couple. But the Others, the irrepressible ones, Tancredi, Clorinda, the lovers of freedom, these two singular creatures, stronger than themselves, yes, the one and the other capable of going, at the price of life, for the love of truth, for love, beyond their own forces, all the way to the other — the farthest, the nearest. The two always-others, who dare to achieve Departure. Even madder and wiser than Torquato Tasso, who created them much freer than himself in a dream. Stranger. Absolutely faithful — to their own human secret — to their own being more-than-man more-than-woman. With courage they do not know themselves, with nobility they do not possess themselves, with humility they do not restrain themselves, do not withold themselves, both agree to surrender themselves, to the point of approaching the other. I no longer know whether my 'they' is masculine or feminine.[1]

What grips me is *the movement* of love. The violently described curve

from a soul to the other body, from a sexed body to another gender of
body, from a smile to a look. *Gracious* exchange (— yes: it is a question of
beautiful *coups de grâce* —) from one pleasure to the other whose sex is
not revealed. It is a question of the grace of genders, instead of the law of
genders, it is a question of dancing, of the aerial crossing of continents. It
is a question in front of Jerusalem, *still only obscurely*, of the mystery of
love which is a question of acrobatics: fly or fall! There are no detours, it
is straight ahead. That is why it is so easy. Yes or No — there is no in-
between. That is why loving is never difficult except in appearance.
Because the opposite of 'easy' is not 'difficult': it is only *impossible*. So the
secret of acrobatics is love? It is confidence, yes: it is the desire to go
across into the other. The body of the acrobat is his soul.

The crossing is vertiginous? Like every crossing. Useless to contem-
plate or fathom what separates: the abyss is always invented by our fear.
We leap and there is grace. Acrobats know: do not look at the separation.
Have eyes, have bodies, only for there, for the other.

Tancredi-is-for-Clorinda-is-for-Tancredi.

If Tancredi is 'lost for love' for Clorinda, it is for Tancredi that he is
lost, but for Clorinda he is more than gained: given.

I wonder: why can only Tancredi love Clorinda? Go as far as her?
Leave the self to go towards the other?

I follow Tancredi and Clorinda through forests, battlefields, the war
between races, religions, over enclosures, chasms, beyond ramparts,
literary genders and others, as far as the wild songs of Rossini.

Then I listen to Tancredi soaring towards his inner Jerusalem borne
along on the hippogriff Music, and returning to us melodiously,
strangely other . . .

For between times, between the unconsciouses, between the stanzas
and measures, from Tasso to Rossini, the story has shifted a little:

Instead of the sumptuous Clorinda, the most impetuous, the most
adorable and vulnerable of knights, there appears a woman of equal
force, but with no other armour than her soul. From out of the armoured
Clorinda has sprung totally unarmed Amenaïde, impregnable as she is so
little threatening, still more powerfully woman, more strongly Clorinda.

And Tancredi? I do not know . . . I hear his (her) voice, its sweetness,
its fury, I hear the high mezzo voice of the Enigma. The Enigma? Yes:
the answer: only Tancredi can love Amenaïde who lives in Clorinda's
breast. Only (s)he.

Only (s)he? Yes. For this Tancredi can only be a Tancred*a*,[2] this is what
Rossini feels and I feel it too, but I do not know how to talk about it.
Because it is the Enigma: it does not explain itself, makes itself heard.

Listen.

I say a Tancreda, I do not say a woman, I could, but nothing is so
simple.

Listen: Rossini does not say that to be Tancredi, the hero, a woman's voice must possess him. He brings it about.

There is no explanation. There is the singing. The body's insistence that in order for a man to love a woman as Tancredi loves Clorinda or Amenaïde, he has to be a woman — I mean Tancredi.

If it is enigmatic, so much the better. Because if it were not we would no longer have the least bit of life work to do.

We have to tour the world and Jerusalem, lose memory, lose knowledge, in order to reach the depths of true love, where we never know when we love, who we love, in whom we love. Tancredi loves Clorinda. Tancredi does not know who in Clorinda is loved by who in him? A moment ago it was a man, a second ago a woman, but was it really that?

One more remark before I lose myself: Clorinda 'knows' that she is a 'woman'. Rossini's Tancred(a) does not: (she) is a Tancredi, only God knows this, and perhaps Rossini a little — as for us, our musical body 'knows' it though we may be unaware of it.

Now I am completely lost. All I have left to offer you is to lead you astray into the space where Tancredi lives and yearns to be a woman.

But I also want to meet a person[3] and to love her beyond true and false which are the two extremes, the ends, the limits of 'reality'.

I want to love a person freely including all of her secrets. I want to love in this person someone that she does not know.

I want to love outside of (the) law: without judgement. Without imposed preference. Does that mean outside of morality? No. Only: without fault. Without false, without true. I want to meet her between the words, beneath language.

I wanted to look at *Tancredi*: magical voices bore me away, whinnying, cooing, far away from myself, far away from us, far away from the opera, to the other side.

I want to meet her intimately, behind gestures, words, activities, in the region of mysteries. Still alone or alone again. And above all uncertain, yes, always already a little strange, because it is only in society and appearance that a person having such depths presents a united, determined surface. But as soon as everyone is gone she hurries into her room and even before changing or removing her make-up she abandons herself with joyous relief to her vital uncertainty, she collapses on the bed like a piece of décor, where she stretches herself and becomes she does not know who once more.

I know that if I start saying 'woman' or 'man' again, and quite simply (as I have done, as we do, as we have all done, which is why I do it too) then I will never be free of the words, nor will she (and we end up by no longer loving who we love, and we deceive ourselves until we no longer love). I would like at least once to try to say what I am trying to think, with difficulty, already, about this question of gender: because I feel that she (this person) must have consciously inflicted it upon herself, at least suffered from it mysteriously. I feel it in the way that she has of throwing herself on her bed as soon as she is alone, as if she were jumping out of someone else, and of stretching herself vigorously and roaring softly, and of rolling over onto her side, and going to sleep for a while. And it is only after a dream that she shudders, and suddenly goes into the bathroom. And looks at herself in the mirror, asks herself, knitting her brows, if it shows on her face, that she does not know. And also, because in the evening she too listens to *Tancredi* while watching the night rising through the window.

So it is a question of the mystery of 'woman' and 'man'. Are they the names of two mysteries or one?

I *feel* the truth of this mystery: mysterious and true. I feel its truth but I do not know how to say it truthfully.

Now musicians have never lost the sense of the mysterious which is the song of truth. What sings in a 'man' is not him, it is her. Have always known it.

But we, who speak, we lose, we lose, I am losing.

But what suffers and rejoices under 'Orpheus' is a woman's-voice.

She listens to Gluck, Mozart and Rossini because they knew too. How to live crying out with frightened joy above the pitfall of words.

Fortunately when someone says 'woman', we still do not know what that means even if we know what we want to say.

And so I wonder what is man and what is woman and what am I, which is what she, in the bathroom, is wondering too, while I no longer know when I say 'a woman' if I am talking about a person you would call 'a woman' or if.

In any case she is not *a* woman. She is plural. Like all living beings, who are sometimes invaded, sometimes populated, incarnated by others, drawing life from others, giving life. Do not know themselves.

And so if I were to talk about a person I met and who has bowled me over, she herself being moved, and I myself moved at seeing her moved, and she feeling me moved, moved in turn, and if this person were a she and a he and a s(he) and a (s)he and a shehe and heshe, I want to be free to tell the truth, I do not want to stop her if she transes,[4] I want him to, I want her to, I will follow them.

And a person who looks like a 'man' full of woman hidden behind this look, what do you call them, and a woman full of woman in whom still another lives, I do not know, and were it not for the look suggesting, and the name, the face make-up and all of the other make-ups . . .

Listen to *Fidelio* again.

Even if I feel clearly that, the more I try to say, the more I feel I have wandered astray far from what, beneath appearances and secretly and obscurely, I am sure I have understood, I think.

I should also say that in order to know it better inside I close my eyes, I avoid looking her straight in the face because it is not impossible that at first sight she may look a little like one of these men who are not at all feminine, but who are capable of this sort of slow inner dance, who have a loving, elastic rapport with the earth and are thus a bit f . . . thus in short a bit m . . . and thus . . .

And then I feel her so clearly and again I know without any doubt how lightly powerful she is like a man who is lightly powerful like a woman who is powerfully light like a man who is gently powerfully powerful like a woman of powerful tenderness . . .

And all that I wanted to try and say is that she is so infinite.

One does not guess anything: one knows.

Before meeting the-one-whose-name-I-still-have-not-spoken, I 'knew' that she listens to *Tancredi*, in the evening, when she is alone, and watches the night falling through the window before her, royal, comes the night draped in her[5] satins of dark blue steel, comes slowly towards her, pensive darkly brilliant, and the armour which covers her only allows her head to be seen; she is a Persian night. She sees her, is amazed by her blacks, by her clouds, by her swirls, and listening to the dark brilliance rising, behind her, from out of the depths of the room, of time, she hears the voice that reigns over her heart, the sea-mother-voice,[6] which was already calling her thirty-five years ago, lulling her, awakening her.

The Third Song in *Jerusalem Delivered* lasts two hours in the hearing and in reality a day and a night. And during all of this time Tancredi and Clorinda do not meet each other, do not meet each other, time almost comes to a halt.

But seen from the top of a fig-tree which overlooks the wall of Solime, the song is contained in these few words:

'The Christian army approaches Solime — Clorinda overpowers the Christians — Tancredi flies to their rescue — Bouillon prepares to attack Solime —'

And between times — Clorinda brushes Tancredi — between the arrows — Tancredi flies — and between the words the earth disappears, time does not have time, Tancredi Clorinda, seen from outside, fly, (but their flight is not rapid enough, time runs out, never, seen from above, will they meet).

But inside the song, God grants them all of the time they need to slip towards one another, all of the time between possibility and impossibility, and inside there is no impossibility, love knows no no, and time does not exist for desire, for the text, or for the unconscious. God gives them the grace to slip in between the sexes alive . . .

When they slipped into this opening, its silence vibrating, in harmony, with the sweet, muted sound of violins, then I saw them.

Tancredi haunted by Clorinda, haunted by Amenaïde, haunted by Sutherland, haunted by Tancredi, haunted by Horne, haunted by Tancredi, and I too enchanted.

Ourselves we do not owe.[7]

I did not see them come in. It was a single apparition for me, but they slipped in as if they had been coming forever or from having forever just taken shape.

I saw them slip in, one all in white, the other all in dark blues, like — not a woman — not a man — not only — like — the personification of the mystery — of humankind — like humanity in person, brooding over its own mystery, which is neither man nor woman of course, which is to begin with two, two people, it is being–itself, with its mystery which is to be a question turned towards the other, and only the other has the answer, has only this answer to give, to the other but not to the self, and this is how I suddenly saw them, slipping down along the same musical question between them a single silence accompanied so softly, and between them the question accorded itself, answered itself, like a question that gives itself to the question that comes forth to meet it, musically grants it the ever sought–after answer.

Because it is only the perfect harmony of two questions that gives an answer.

That is why there are so few answers in the world, there are so many questions, and so many books, so much hope, and despairing, and so many traces of error, but music, so little, and answers occurring, with the questions perching on their laps, eyes closed, listening, listening, there are so few. Because only two questions in perfect harmony end up composing an answer: that is, two questions moving toward one another with the same sustained rhythm, like two arrows shot forth at the same moment by two equal archers from the two sides of the mountain ascending like two alto voices soaring from the two shores of the sea above the orchestra will perhaps end up meeting above the summit, if a storm does not intervene. A storm, or history.

But first the chance of the answer is a question of body. Then of culture, history, and all the rest. And in the end the truth is perhaps that the only questions that harmonize to compose an answer had begun to answer from the start, had perhaps never even turned toward each other asking, but already committing and giving themselves to each other, had already begun to rise up in reply, up through the air along the slopes like a bird perching on the arrow, and on the other side, this unparalleled thing has occurred as well, so that when the arrows at the height of their trajectory obey the laws of physics, the two birds catch sight of each other from a distance, and free, meet each other above the clouds where we can no longer see them but we can hear their triumphant cry very clearly.

To return to my two precious apparitions, to tell the truth, as soon as I saw them, gliding toward one another, because of the suppleness of their movement, I guessed. Perhaps because of their look of astonishment, gently astonished, remaining astonished, as if to greet one another close up as well as from far away? Gliding, yes, all in whites, one shining forth to meet the other all shimmering in deep blues, and the whites too created a depth, a density, like two fates: as if they felt each other inevitable. Not like a woman walks and, graceful or awkward she is woman–walking, and it was not a man who was advancing, not simply man-approaching, who came. No, before me, they slipped, like two boats gliding over the water, as if at the mercy of the other. Drawn to each other, beholding each other with one imperceptible movement, fell lightly, with their whole body, holding each other with their eyes, holding back with a look from the brim of their eyes, wondering, asking: why me? In the same sweet silence accompanied by twelve violins, thinking the whole time, astonished, not speaking, as if they were thinking that this was the last time they would be able to look at each other and question each other, and still not know who me? Why me? Who? Me who . . .

Why me? Standing, very close now, both the same height, they could have touched, there was hardly any astonishment left now, but they continued to be astonished, 'why am I in white, and the other coming night-blue to meet the day' . . .

'Why', they ask one another giving themselves as an answer, draped in many silks, and the astonishment swells their breasts, with their whole body asking each other and saying: 'because it's you' and the musical harmony of the astonishments is the answer.

(I realize that I am postponing the task of deciding to make the evidence visible. I am afraid, I will not hide it, because I have a secret to tell which is so beautiful that it dazzled me and if I am not able to dazzle you, I will have committed a crime against everything that I venerate, life, beauty, desire. Because one must reveal the secrets, but in their splendour. Otherwise, if one repeats without dazzling, one violates the secret of the secret, it is sexuality without God. Do I have enough strength to raise the secret of this story above my head? Do I have the heroic serenity, the male feminity — these are the virtues that a respect for my vision requires.)

I follow them . . .

So high, painfully trying to give herself to Tancredi, Amenaïde is no more than a look, ah! she would like to die with her eyes open, her look never leaving his eyes, fade away in his night like the sun and Tancredi in the same astonishment is no more than a pair of eyes, and, for a fraction of a second, together, they nearly die, they forget the world and slip into eternity.

I see them then from very close up, I see their madness, their secret:

He was the most beautiful of a woman, he was the most majestic of women, he was radiant with the majesty of a woman.

And more beautiful than a young man, more beautiful than a knight of faith, she was noble with the power of a hero.

He the most proudly erotic of wild creatures.

She pitiless passion, the inexorable bravery of love:

It is thus. What I saw and they saw it too.

Why me? were struggling now as if they were going to enter each other.

And the weapons signify: I beg of you conquer me but do not wound me.

Slip towards one another like night towards the day.

Tancredi falls like the night, high, full of dreams, and so profound and all ice on the outside but his heart burns, like the night which adores and does not know itself.

Falls large and delicate and male on the outside but under the dark blue star-studded armour, reigns the burning humility of a mistress.

And what I saw, blazing Amenaïde sees it too, even if her apparel eclipses the white of the snow crowning the summit of the Alps, her pride is only the measure of her profound humility, if he is mistress, she is male-lover . . .

This is what I wanted to say.

In a dream I saw a pure turquoise. Sobbing I reach out trying to grasp it. It is in the middle of the sky. It is above my life like my own external heart. I want it, I see it, I want it the way that Tancredi wants his beloved or alive wants her alive even unto death, the way human beings need the secret of their own life. I see it shining, the splendour of my existence, my external treasure, I see above my head the meaning of my whole history. A single night separates me from it. I try to cross it. I hold out my hands, I am sobbing with rage, I have it right at my finger tips.

The sky is near only one transparent night to cross.

Inside the turquoise gleams a fascinating pearl.

My life burns in order to rise above itself towards my secret. I burn my
soul so that a flame will rise higher, nearer, than me, but what rises
highest higher nearer the turquoise is the smoke, and my eyes full of
tears I sob with hope.

The why of my life is a turquoise that I could hold in my right hand. I
burn for a tiny double star. Because it is so infinitely pure. My secret is
the star of the Evidence. At the heart of it lies a soft gleaming pearl like
the flash of eternity at the heart of a moment. My star that still has no
name!
   My secret is no bigger than a hazel-nut of eternity.
   Only one night still holds back my hand.
   I see what my turquoise means. A dark blue silence before my lips
holds back my words in a nebula.
   My turquoise contains its most precious part. An opaque pearl is the
secret of its transparency. The secret of the royal blue is the infinite
whiteness of its depth.
   I can only sob what I wanted to say.
   Tancredi leant forward, asking himself so blue slowly as if they were
looking at one another for the last time from so far away why are you so
white looking so closely at one another, more closely as an adored
woman looks in the mirror in search of the secret of this love, asking it
who is loved, asking herself who she is, the one who in me is adored,
does not look at herself, tries to discover the secret that the other
cherishes, looks painfully beneath her own features for the soul of the
other, as high and noble and silent Amenaïde favoured by the night
glides along and her heart burns contemplating the why of her life which
shines blue, attracts her and answers her royally mysteriously blue and so
near why are you so blue?
   I ask myself: will I one day understand the secret of this love which I
feel and which at the touch of my fingers, at the touch of my words, fades
away: Will I one day understand the night? Will I know who understands
me?
   I saw their secret. What I am telling of it is no more than light turned to
dust. He was so handsome one felt he was beautiful. And she was not
only a beautiful woman, she was handsome: I am telling what one could
see:

> The two of them come swooping down on each other like
>   two enemies.
> Want to take the measure of each other, urged on by desire,
>   have elected each other,
> In the darkness do not meet

(At this point an outburst of song shook the night, and I scribbled down all that I heard, breathless phrases, on bits of paper, eyes on them, hand noting blindly):

Night day both he and she[8]
Spring forth, still don't meet
What do you want of me, what are you bringing me
Leave you I'd rather die
Why were you searching for me, me, so ardently
As if you knew me
As if I knew you
My fiancée I beg you to tell me your name
Since fate, since destiny have so ordained
I will not reveal my name, my real name
As if you knew me
Open their arms and spring forth
If it were war they would not miss each other,
But it's not war, it's love, they brush one another
Do not embrace, it's the war of love
Let her breathe if he can
You are no longer my sister
I am no longer your child
The anger and darkness are neither feigned nor measured
Their feet are immobile, but their souls are restless, excited, the
    swords come down, broadside, or point first,
What are you fleeing my love? Standing together. Do not see each
    other . . .
Nothing separates them,
What separates them? The dark malice of History
The struggle forces them closer and closer,
Already they can't use the point anymore,
They blind one another with looks
Three times Amenaïde receives Tancredi's look
Three times she breaks free from this attraction she fears
Believe you I'd rather die
But with my whole life in spite of myself I believe you
You are no longer my child
I am no longer your sister.
Finally exhausted, they draw back to breathe for a moment attentive
    and silent like two adversaries
Asking themselves, who will vanquish, love, death . . .
Then what sweetness when all pain is exhausted
When anger no longer has any blood, anguish is no longer sustained
Then what respect.

I do not see what could separate them. Two beings made one for the other, apparently neither sister nor brother and nevertheless of equal measure and equally without measure.

One can see that they are attuned to each other in every way, like a royal soprano to an alto capable of the highest notes, one can see that they are a match for each other in differences and in likenesses the one enhances and brightens the other. The two of them equal in stature, in power, in richness of soul, in mobility of spirit, equal in virtue and different in feature, in colour, in resonance, like . . . like Sutherland and Horne for example.

One can see nothing separating them. Only an imperceptible vibration. A delay, as in life.

Will they end up lips upon lips by taking each other and breathing life into each other again? I still think so. If not it would truly be a misfortune.

I was vaguely afraid. There was such a light trembling in their breathing. As if they were silently struggling together against a word, a single terrible word, with all of their forces turned inwardly, leaning over the wall, afraid of being surprised by an enemy who was unique but as powerful and cunning as poison, who would not come from the present, but who could escape like jealousy itself, from a very ancient and unhappy time.

But thus occupied in not letting themselves be surprised by the infernal word, they had not yet had the sweet leisure to say I love you.

Now they look at each other a little breathlessly, begging each other with their eyes with a tenderness that would turn a lioness into a faithful ally, and lean on their swords their bodies exhausted.

Yet, with the impossible in between them, do not leave each other
The impossible unites them like the night
In which lose and find themselves and each other
Amie! In your cruel destiny I will remain faithful to you
Why should it be impossible? Because it was night? Because it was
  day? Why shouldn't it be possible?
Amie in your faithful destiny I will remain cruel to you.

(And yet I felt vaguely that they were still searching, either one was too heavy or the other was losing a lightness. I don't know who said,

I should embrace her	I can't
I should confront her	I can't
I should flee from her.[9]	

I do not want to know who could not help fleeing, could not help falling.

Was it misfortune? The truth is that there was mistrust. But that was in another story.)

So I do not know who I started to love all of a sudden with all the weight of my own desire insisting, in vain. I was in love with one with the other. With both of them. Because of the other I loved. One because the other. One for and against the other.

Yes she is the object of my passion
The object of my suffering is she,
This slow passion which threatens one towards the other
This tormenting hope, all growing in my heart,
This apprehension, this confidence,
This wonder, all growing
This belief, this non-belief,
This passion which grieves my heart and enchants me,
It is she too, that I adore, I don't know why,
Love surprised me as I was watching
Two great persons look at each other for the last time,
Caught hold of me in her big, strong but delicate arms
And I fell, astonished,
In love,
Not just with the one that I wanted to love,
That I loved in advance, because she was blue and dark
And ardent and profound like someone I'd loved before
But astonished, I too fell into the musical aura
Of the one that I wasn't thinking about, the other, the white and gold,
The pure and confident and spontaneous one, she too
At the last moment, and because one was the answer that the other
    didn't dare hope for and with all her soul humbly hoped for,

Each amplifies the other, each is magnified by the other. Each all the greater and more magnificent for mysteriously understanding the other.

Is Tancredi a woman who is ending or a man who is beginning to be a woman in order to be a man?

But my God, I am only me, I am only a woman, how can I express what is more than me? I divine what is more than a woman, what is more than a man, but above me, everything sparkles and dazzles me and merges into a single person with athletic aspirations, rather tall for a woman, yes she seems to me to be a woman but set naturally in the bearing of a man, like my pearl in my turquoise.

What do you call a person[10] who looks rather more like a woman with dark blue eyes, with an icy look in appearance and who is burning inside, who is large and imposing like the night and stars nuzzle up against her full breast, closing their eyes in love, who fights like a hero, would give up her life like a mother, and who sheds tears of impatience and grief, and who dreams only of love as a destiny, and who takes fortresses more easily than a kiss, and her voice is so deep and warm and moist, it sounds like the sea of human tears and every woman not bound by the ties of marriage, who hears it, feels the burning need to immerse herself in it?

In this story she bore the name of Tancredi, his past, his arms. Help Mozart, Rossini, help number without gender, gender without limit!

When does woman begin when does one become other when continues when pursues when finally touches finally embraces?

. . . No; I should rather ask;

Where does man begin woman begin continue?

Continues

Yet — Already the last stars are paling with the first fires of dawn and yet the struggle continues.

This Tancredi was worried about the fatal triumph;

Continued in an alto voice, in which I wanted to pour all my tears:

Must I surrender? Must I conquer? Who?

Who are you, I beg you, Victor or Vanquished, tell me, I will know who I save, who I lose.

Speak to me: I am not listening to you: Speak to me.

You alone have been loved by my heart.

How can I help but believe you.

Only I must believe the impossible,

So farewell.

What do you want? To leave you. To follow you.

Two fighters. Two adversaries before each other against the impossible

Yes you are the object of my suffering

Don't strike each other. Contemplate each other.

Turn from each other. Flee from each other

As if they were falling upon one another.

(There are several Tancredis, which is why I'm having such a hard time trying not to mislead us. I promise that I will do my utmost as soon as broad daylight arrives to explain myself on this subject.)

I feel clearly that I am inside of the night and yet before my own night. feel that I am before the mystery, which I am destined to encounter and not to resolve. This Tancredi, this Amenaïde, these first two, are the figures of my mystery. Everything that I write, it seems to me, leads me myopically to their embraces, and then I feel that everything is happening right there before my hopelessly wonderstruck eyes, the meaning of the mystery catches on fire, a cry explodes in my breast — as if I were 'discovering' 'the truth' of 'love' (all of these words are smoke choking the pure point of my cry) — and — fiat *nox*!

But perhaps what is hardest and most necessary, is to positively forget these judges who make us answer their stupid summons stupidly, justify the non-justifiable, speak silence, crush the music under the millstone of words, lie by swearing to tell only their truth, plead guilty to a lack of absence and to a lack of weakness, make excuses for every thought, to positively forget, in other words to forget them fearlessly, with a bound to quicken the pace, without ever really forgetting them, to fling a glistening forgetfulness over our shoulders and to run till we reach the zone of free souls, where they cannot venture because they perish on contact with the pure air.

After our oppressive and inflexible era, I would like to live in a time in which language would not be bound, castrated, intimidated, obliged to obey the false scholars who are true ignoramuses.

But sometimes I am stopped by the word-police, searched, interrogated and counter-interrogated. Sometimes I am the one who stops; thinking perhaps mistakenly, that I must all the same show that I am not afraid of the insults hurled at us. I turn around, I answer and the struggle begins, to the cries of Women! Women! hurled out, picked up in hatred, in love. In the din of the arguments one no longer knows what one is attacking, what one is defending, the words change in value depending on the speakers, now blessings, now curses.

I know perfectly well that the best way to defend a truth is to never pronounce its name, to never expose it to public abuse. Through constant repetition, the word 'Jew' becomes as dry as a fossil. (It is the same with the word 'true', which is accused, in our olden times, of being too good to be true.)

And nowadays there are so many clandestine massacres of women that a woman has to say 'woman' a dozen times a day in order to protest.

But by constantly saying 'I am a woman', we end by creating a sort of forced truth. And the worst of it is that the more we say it, to avoid being swept along by the current far away from the native shores the more securely we moor ourselves to avoid being separated, the more we contribute to reinforcing the limitations of the forces, to restricting the native territories and to fortifying the prejudices. We are closed in, we enclose ourselves, we enwoman ourselves.[11] And the worst of it is that what was the sweet and inexplicable and intimate truth, the magic hand on the heart, beneath which we could faint with joy, becomes a phrase.

So the truth, which appears inside the night, in the warm depths of a dream, and then only, peacefully undresses before me and smiling comes slipping I do not know how over my innermost body, and caresses my heart, and — then — the sweet softness of her[12] breasts — that is what absolute knowledge is — if what I am writing is not clear enough, this is normal, since not a single word ever returns from the luminous depths where our truth lives. The few words that come close are turned into sighs — so, the truth which only lives sheltered by silence, is forced to

appear, and then she is like a fish out of water, thinking in a final
convulsion of the sea, then, the end.

But in this night full of voices, I am bewildered between two
Tancredis. Is the one the other or the same or the hidden truth or the
manifest truth of the other? Here I am between one and the other,
astonished, stubbornly refusing to take my eyes off the mystery: as if I
wanted to become conscious of my unconscious into which I dive. Here
I am under the sea with my lantern. I circle around inside a question, like
a Chinese fish in a swimming pool. I am here and I am all at sea: I
imagine that there is an answer outside.
'Why is it necessary for this Tancredi to be a Tancreda?'

But there is no outside. My swimming pool is infinite. It is the world.

Let us not think. Let us swim.

There are two Tancredis. They are not altogether the same, are almost
the same. Tancredi of Jerusalem is he Tancredi of Syracuse or is she not?
It is because he insisted on knowing what he was thinking that
Tancredi turned back against himself in a final and furious effort in order
to come to grips with himself.

These are things to dream of.

I am swimming between two Tancredis, the water is almost a night
starred with serenity. I am dreaming along in the very substance of
eroticism, as if music had finally once more become what it was, musical
wave. I am swimming between little waves of thoughts.
The enigma is fresh inside, I feel good here, love slips and continues,
from Jerusalem to Syracuse and turns back again, the appearance
changes and reality blushes with emotion.
First of all it is the story of a Tancredi who loves a hero who is a
woman who is in reality a hero who is a woman and if he loves her it is
because she is a woman. And so is he.
There is a Clorinda, who is a woman who has the strength to have the
bearing of a man and who is all the more one because the other. Finally, I
am not sure. And so Tancredi is the person who loves this woman.
So Rossini guesses: for a man to love as Tancredi loves this woman
who is this and still more, he had to be a woman.
I am lost . . .
So much the better . . . Tancredi can only be a woman when he is a
man. Or no? Tancredi can only be a woman when she is a man?
A-man-who-loves-a-woman-as-if-he-were-a-woman — has a voice
which traverses life, death, walls, sands, superstitions, magnificent

armour, shields, images, languages, meanings, neither race nor colour nor one gender, nor another gender, hold it captive, it is made to celebrate she who inspires it. Tancredi sings a woman: a woman sings Tancredi . . .

Tancredi, a woman . . .

If I love a woman I will call her Tancredi.

Astonished Tancredi astonished Tancreda understands Clorinda, and for Rossini, it is obvious, 'Tancredi' is a woman in a man.

But for the Christians and for all of Jerusalem, it is Clorinda who is a woman in a man.

And here I see them spring forth towards each other more rapidly than I can look, and swoop down and their steeds raise a cloud of bright dust, I can no longer see them, I can only hear the voices measuring each other, the lioness springing, the eagle rending the air; I can hear two voices, one is a woman's and the other one is a woman's too, rushing headlong towards one another, one of them is not a woman, one of them is not only a woman, one is not only the opposite of the other.

What a secret!
O heaven you know for whom I tremble
Because he doesn't know who she is
Doesn't know he is a woman
Because with what difference
She is a woman, heaven knows,
What is the difference? It isn't only the sex,
It's the way that love loves, above walls, despite armour, after the end
    of the world,
But I don't know how to say it.
I hear the alto wondering who
Her vast clear night full of tears
Trembles soprano and breaks up there
And falls again
And at once regains breath and escapes all my questions which hold
    me below.
Higher up, the questions don't follow, there are only answers
Which is why women's voices are so joyful and free.

The word 'woman' holds me captive. I would like to wear it out, to lose it, and to continue along on the trail of She who lives without this great worry.

All the more lovable for being more woman all the more man for being more woman and perhaps all the more woman . . .

If I loved a woman I would call her with my voice still moist and salty, Tancredi my Beloved.[13]

Notes

1. In the French, literally 'I no longer know whether I should say they ('ils') or they ('elles')'. The problem here refers to the fact that, in French, 'they' is *either* masculine (*ils*) *or* feminine (*elles*), the masculine taking precedence over the feminine whenever the 'they' includes so much as a single masculine element. As elsewhere in the text, much of the grammatical echoing of the question of sexual gender is unfortunately lost in the English translation.
2. The feminine is emphasized in the French through the underlined use of the feminine indefinite article '*une* Tancrède'.
3. In French, the word 'person' (*personne*) is feminine and thus requires the corresponding feminine pronouns and adjectives in agreement. This enables the author to leave the question of the sexual gender of this 'person' in suspense, while insisting on the feminine at the grammatical level. As this possibility does not exist in English, where it is a question of either/or, we have chosen here as elsewhere to translate 'person' in the feminine.
4. The verb '*transe(r)*' is an invention by the author, combining the Latin prefix *trans-* (across, beyond, on or to the other side) with the French noun *transe* which signifies both 'trance' and 'a state of being "beside oneself"'.
5. In French 'the night' (*la nuit*) is feminine.
6. The play on words is between *mer* (m.), 'sea' and its homophone *mère* (f.), 'mother'.
7. The quotation (from *Twelfth Night*, Act 1, scene 5) is given in English in the original text.
8. In French 'night' (*la nuit*) is feminine, while 'day' (*le jour*) is masculine.
9. In the French the gender of the object pronoun is only recognizable in the last of these three lines.
10. 'Person' is feminine in French (see note 3 above).
11. The verb *enfemme(r)* is an invention by the author, placing the word for 'woman' — *femme* — within the French verb *enfermer* — 'to enclose'.
12. In French 'the truth' (*la vérité*) is feminine.
13. 'Tancredi continues' first appeared as 'Tancrède continue' in *Etudes Freudiennes*, Nos 21–22, Paris, March 1983, pp. 115–31.

4

Let's go to the fountain:
on George Sand and writing

Anne Berger

(This essay is a revised version of a lecture given in French at the Seventh International George Sand Conference in October 1986. The full transcript of this lecture can be found in the forthcoming volume of Conference Proceedings to be published by the Greenwood Press in the USA. Anne Berger wishes to thank James T. Siegel for his help in translating her essay.)

George Sand wrote her autobiography and a series of novels of country life during the same period. Having gone through a double apprenticeship in the art of living and writing, she decided, in the late 1840s, to tell the story of her life. She no longer needed, at that point, to learn in order to live. She had 'reached an age of tranquility when her personality had nothing to gain by displaying itself'. She no longer 'sought the key words'.[1] It was when she ceased to believe that the subject could grasp itself through speculation that she undertook to 'communicate herself' to others in a pedagogical and maternal gesture. At this moment, she definitively assumed the position of the artist, identifying herself with a destiny which she neither foresaw nor wanted, tying the thread of her life to the thread of the text. It was as an artist that she proceeded to reveal a reality without which the teaching provided by fiction remained, according to her, incomplete. But, she said: 'It is costly for an artist to touch on this reality . . . it is not, without a great effort that I *will descend into the prose of my subject* (added emphasis).[2]

Thus the novels of country life coincide with her accession to the peak of art. From this point, the artist then undertakes a difficult descent in order to once again touch the reality of 'his' subject, indeed of *the* subject.

George Sand's aesthetic concerns in the prefaces to her rustic novels seem to display the success of her ascent. Indeed she comes close to formulating an aesthetic theory when she examines the complex connections between art and nature on the one hand and art and history on the other. The degree to which she idealizes her rustic characters adds further evidence. Idealization is an essential part of artistic representation and activity, as she repeatedly stresses.[3] Finally, the apparent lack of autobiographical concern in her rustic novels at the moment when *The Story of My Life* is written contrasts with the extensive use of personal material in her other novels. (The personal stance in the prefaces to her other novels, such as *Lelia*, *Indiana* or *Mauprat*, accounts for their ideological cast as well as their tone, which is either apologetic or polemic.)

If the novels of country life seem to assume a stance at odds with the prosaic reality of her subject, they are at the same time the most singular and most accomplished expression of her artistic language. Whereas George Sand often indulges in the novelistic conventions of her time by offering the reader a mixture of realistic description and 'Rocamboles-que' adventures, she has an entirely different purpose in her 'études champêtres'.[4] Condemning the novelistic production of her time as an unfortunate offspring of bourgeois ideology, she presents the rustic novel as a reversal of the contemporary novel which delights in the disfiguration of reality[5] and uses the pen as a 'dagger' in the services of a 'brutal and fiery art'.

George Sand opposes the study of the quiet 'mystery of primitive simplicity' to the violence of bourgeois representation. Indeed, she writes most of her rustic novels in Nohant, her native village, far from the tumults of history and the seductions of society. She will return there more and more often in the second and non-written part of her life. In this sense, she departs from the implacable law, epitomized in Balzac's novels, which governs the course of all social and artistic education. This law commands a break with native land and attachments. It demands that artistic success be defined through social accomplishment, the symbol of which is the conquest of Paris.[6] On the contrary, artistic maturation seems to coincide for George Sand with a return to her original location. I would also like to read this return as an attempt to recover her own language. George Sand does not intend to revive the aristocratic tradition of the 'pastoral'[7] whose idyllic representations are obviously part of an idealistic denial, if not a refusal, of history. She dismisses both the parricidal dagger of the bourgeoisie and the shepherd's crook of Marie-Antoinette. Indeed, her rustic novels, with the exception of *Jeanne*, have some features in common with fairy tales: all is well that ends well; obstacles (such as the money problems which threaten the story with the phantom of bourgeois society) are magically overcome; marriage sanctifies the abolition of the contradictions and rifts imposed by history. However, even if she explicitly resorts to the strategies of fairy tales, George Sand insists on the truth of her endeavour. François

Rollinat, her friend and the interlocutor of her preface to *François le Champi*, recalls that the priest's housekeeper and the man who twines hemp told them a 'true story':

> 'Between the two of them they told us a true story, rather long, which looked like an intimate novel. Do you remember it?'
> 'Perfectly, and I could retell it word for word in their language.'[8]

At the end of the novel, someone who has just heard the story echoes Rollinat's remark:

> 'Then the story is completely true?' Sylvine Courtioux asked.
> 'If it isn't, it could well be', answered the twiner of hemp. 'And if you don't believe me, go and see for yourself.'[9]

Thus the 'truth' of its narrative conditions guarantees the truthfulness of the rustic tale. It is a true story because it is directly recounted by real peasants. All the difficulty and originality of George Sand's project lie in her desire to make the language of peasants heard. Ethnographic critics have tried to determine the extent to which she was faithful to this project. She has been declared faithful because her tale is studded with regional Berrichon expressions and unfaithful because she occasionally invented such expressions.

The contradictory necessity of faithfulness and unfaithfulness to the peasant language is precisely the central issue. The peasant mode of expression is fundamentally oral. The relation of 'our literature' — which 'only knows how to amplify or disguise' — to 'rustic songs, narratives and tales'[10] emblematizes the relation of written to oral language. Since we learn to speak before we learn to read or write, the passage to writing can be experienced as a shift to a second language. In any case, it opens a division internal to linguistic practice: it requires translation, inevitably unfaithful. It provokes a defiant distancing, if not the total obliteration of all traces of an orality improper to the code of writing. Therefore, although George Sand is able to 'recount word for word in their language' François le Champi's story as it was told by the peasants, she must translate it from the moment she writes it down: 'Their language demands to be translated; one has to write in French and not allow oneself any word that is not unless it is so intelligible that a footnote would be useless for the reader.'[11]

What should then be found in the rustic novels is a way to articulate a language doubly primitive and thus doubly menaced by disappearance: primitive or primary because it is oral and primitive because it is spoken by the most primitive layer of society.

I want rapidly to list the linguistic devices which, by emphasizing the primacy of the oral, enable George Sand to be faithful to peasant language. She particularly likes to place the narration in the mouths of peasants, a device she uses in other novels as well. Even in the case of *Jeanne*, the first and least strictly rustic of her rustic novels, where the sad fate of the heroine could be linked to the failure to restore an original language,[12] she invents the following dedication:

> To Françoise Meillant
> You cannot read, my quiet friend. But your daughter and mine have been to school. Some day, at a gathering on a winter evening, while you spin, they will tell you the story which will become much prettier by passing through their mouths.[13]

Despite the denaturing quality of writing, the possibility of passing the tale through the mouths of the daughters to the mother might save, if not Jeanne, at least her story. The great importance granted to dialogue in George Sand's novels as well as in all her writings — for example, her insistence on considering written correspondence as 'chatter'[14] — seems to me another indication of her desire to inscribe or represent orality.

Dialogue represents the simplest form of oral communication. It also functions as a main diegetic tool in her novels. Whether we think of the dialogue between the narrator and 'his' friend in the prefaces to *François le Champi* and *La petite Fadette* or of the dialogues between François and Madeleine, Landry and Fadette, Bernard and Edmée, or even She and Him in the novel of that name, in every case their maieutic virtue is essential to the development of the story. Every time women speak, with the exception of the prefaces where the male-friend plays the role of initiator and maieutician, it allows the other to give birth to his own speech. The dialogue guarantees his coming to the world; introspection is practically non-existent in the rustic novels. When it does occur, it means that received speech is interiorized. Above all, dialogue is the royal path of love; through it the essence of love manifests itself. Landry falls in love with the speech of 'la petite Fadette' at a moment when the two find themselves outside the social scene. It is just at the point in 'la petite Fadette''s speech when she tells him that she takes care of her little brother as though she were his mother[15] (thus revealing the maternal figure hidden under her rags and her boyishness), that Landry falls madly in love with her. In a similar way, one could read the story of François le Champi as another instance of love at first speech. It tells of the coming to speech, thanks to Madeleine, of a poor nameless child who 'did not know how to say a word'. By addressing herself to him and by loving him, Madeleine literally gives him speech.

In *The Story of My Life* George Sand associates the moment when she was forced by her paternal grandmother to stop speaking the Berrichon patois with her mother's departure. The grandmother forced the mother to leave after the death of their common love object, Maurice Dupin, George Sand's father. She provided her granddaughter with a second education, following the primary education under the mother's guidance, which George Sand describes as an attempt to break original ties. Thus began a period of suppression which she evokes in these terms:

> She (the grandmother) was eager to cast off my inveterate sloppiness which my mother had never bothered to correct. I wasn't to roll on the ground any more, or to laugh so loud, or to talk our broad Berrichon dialect.[16]

The repression of the mother coincides with the prohibition of Berrichon.

The distance between the 'base' and the 'summit', between *The Story of My Life* and the Berrichon novels, between 'the reality of the subject' and the artistic ideal, is clearly marked. However, perhaps one could say that, reaching the summit of art, George Sand directs herself toward the mother's tongue as though it were the living source of her artistic language.

The statement which opens the actual narrative of *The Story of My Life* is often forgotten:

> One is not only one's father's child, *one is also a bit, I believe, one's mother's*. It seems to me one is even more so; we are held to the womb which bore us in the most immediate, powerful and sacred way (added emphasis).[17]

This phrase is forgotten because it emerges with such pain, and comes with such reticence before it affirms itself. By contrast one does not forget, particularly if one is a critic by profession, this other sentence, which is so assertive: 'I will go on with my father's story since he is, without punning, the real author of the story of my life.'[18] It resonates all the more in memory since *The Story of My Life* indeed begins with the story of George Sand's father. Moreover the word 'author' seems to clearly establish the symbolic affiliation between 'the author of life' (l'auteur de ses jours') and the author of novels. It has always been easier, and this was even more true then, to have oneself recognized as the child of one's father.

But were we to look more closely, we could avoid a precipitous interpretation which would make George Sand, a writer with a masculine pseudonym, the worthy daughter, if not the son, of her father, Maurice. For the story of the father George Sand recounts so ardently is in fact the marvellous story of a mother and a son and their reciprocal passion. Maurice, the beloved and loving son, later displayed these treasures of love transmitted to him by his mother for Sophie-Victoire, mother of George Sand. A woman of the people, older than him, Sophie-Victoire could have matched the revolutionary ideals of his mother if the latter had not been jealous of her. He remained faithful to the mother, from then on torn between two loyalties which were one in their origin. I would like to recall two important moments in George Sand's narrative. In the first, she evokes Maurice's voluntary enlistment in the service of the Revolution while his mother was in gaol during the Terror:

> Although suffering from the Revolution in his very entrails because he felt his adored mother under the knife, I never see him curse the Mother–ideas ('les Idées mères') of the Revolution.[19]

Maurice Dupin is faithful to the maternal principle even when it entails contradiction.

The second moment seems to me most significant. It follows the recounting of a heartrending separation, again provoked by revolutionary events:

> This poor child had never left his mother, he had never known, never foreseen pain. *He was as beautiful as a flower and as chaste as a maid.* He was sixteen . . . *At that age, a boy raised by a tender mother is an exceptional being in creation. He belongs, so to speak, to no gender. He loves his mother in a way a daughter does not love her* and will never be able to love her. Drowned in the bliss of being exclusively loved and adoringly cherished, this mother is the object of a kind of cult for him. This is love without the storms and the faults he will be dragged into later by love for another woman. Yes, this is ideal love, and it lasts only a moment in a man's life (added emphasis).[20]

Thus the ideal son is indeed a daughter; the loving son represents the ideal daughter of the mother, the one George Sand did not have but the one she was herself. It is in this way that George Sand identifies herself with her father; not with a paternal figure but with the son of the mother, even of two mothers. For, George Sand adds, if he is 'capable of ardently and nobly loving a new idol' (his wife), it is because 'he will have gone through the sacred apprenticeship of true love with his mother'. Was not George Sand the adored and adoring daughter of her own mother and the 'son' of her grandmother, who recognized in her the living image of her late son? After a few sentences the story that George Sand tells us ceases to be strictly biographical and turns into a subjectless reverie, a prelude to a novelistic creation.[21] Can one not recognize in this narrative the very story of *François le Champi* that George Sand started to write in 1847, the year she started to put down her own story? Does not François le Champi, with his 'mother' Madeleine, experience the sacred apprenticeship of a true and ideal love? Nothing is more sublime, indeed more sublimated, than this novel of love, the most perfect and the least erotic of all romantic novels. It tells the story of a son 'as well behaved as a good girl',[22] endowed with the extraordinary capacity to act as the mother in his turn. He takes care of Madeleine in all the ways she took care of him; he looks after the house, he cures her and feeds her. This story could well represent the originary scene of George Sand's fantasy since this term relates the realm of the poetic to the unconscious. In *François le Champi* one finds the primary system of the writer's ego-identifications as well as the source of her romantic imagination. 'In my opinion', she writes as a conclusion to her description of this sacred apprenticeship, 'poets and novelists have not sufficiently recognized this observable topic, this swift and unique moment in the life of a man, which is a source of poetry.' Then she interrupts the dream-story of a father eternally kept by death in the guise of a young man, a faithful lover and faithfully loved, with the exclamation: This existence would have made such a beautiful topic for a novel, had not the principal characters been my father, my mother and my grandmother!'[23] I leave George Sand with her paraliptical statement. I will only note that it could lead us to rethink the connections between the biographical and the novelist in her work. Whether it concerns Maurice Dupin, George Sand herself, or Maurice Sand, the son who took his mother's name, what she tells is indeed the story of the mother's child. For the first two characters of this intimate novel, it is a story about the restoration of ties broken by history. Is not history itself the sad account of innumerable separations?

George Sand describes the catastrophic separation, inevitable in our cultural system, which initiates the historical process, precisely as a separation from original language. In the passage we are concerned with, she engages in a diatribe against the damage of the second education, the education the boy gets no longer from his mother but at school. The school-boy becomes ugly, he begins to fear women, 'his mother's caresses make him blush,' 'the most beautiful languages of the world', those of the poets, disgust him. And, George Sand concludes,

> It will take him years to lose the fruit of his detestable education, *to learn his own language*, forgetting the Latin he hardly knows and the Greek he does not know at all, so he can form his taste and have the right idea of history ... *Only then will he love his mother*. But the passions instantly seize him and he will never have known this heavenly love I was talking about, which is like a pause for a man's soul in the bosom of an enchanting oasis (added emphasis).[24]

Thus the writer advocates a third moment of apprenticeship aimed at unlearning the lessons of the social in order to recover the taste of one's own tongue. In my opinion, this educational project is the most subtle and the most revolutionary aspect of George Sand's thought. She does not conceive of the return to the mother as a regression to a state of nature, a recrossing of the threshold of language acquisition. Rather she thinks of it as a passage beyond divisions (nature/culture, body/language) created precisely by placing the mother outside the socio-cultural order.

Contrary to what a Lacanian or Kristevan analysis would have us believe, in George Sand's life and work it is the mother who guarantees access to the symbolic order and the maintenance of meaning through the gift of speech made to the child. As evidence, I want to refer the reader to the many anecdotes of language acquisition told by George Sand in *The Story of My Life*. They are all connected with the mother, whether they concern the first utterance of the verb 'to love' or the endless fairy tales little Aurore invents for her mother. The latter, 'a natural artist', helps her daughter keep hold of the thread of her speech. I would add to these examples the reading lessons in her novels. In *Mauprat*, for instance, Patience learns how to read poetry under the direction of the maternal Edmée. Madeleine teaches François how to read in *François le Champi*; the fact that she can read is considered her most striking feature by the peasant narrators. The scene of the reading lesson always shows two people reading aloud, as when the mother reads her child a bedtime story, like the story of François le Champi that Proust's mother tells him in a voice which penetrates him forever. Thus the dimension of speech is maintained and founds the pleasure of consuming the book in the union of mouths and ears. Through speech, both the primitive maternal and the cultural, pleasure and the production of meaning, are linked. Thus the 'problem' Lacan evokes for us might be addressed. 'The problem is that of the relationship in the subject between speech and language':[25] 'speech', by which the subject believes he expresses himself as the subject of his desire, and 'language', which, by separating the subject from his own body, abolishes desire as it sanctions it. 'Speech indeed is a gift of language', Lacan writes. But if 'in the gift of speech resides all the reality of its effects'[26] still Lacan gives us no indication of how we are to consider the gift. He does not qualify the gift; he does not say 'who' gives. Rather he suggests that language gives itself, that the Word, in enunciating itself, makes a present of itself, just as the law, God, or the analyst according to Lacan, do. But if Lacan is right to say that the *gift* of speech, by generating transference, founds the 'efficacy of linguistic symbols', is not what gives or what provokes giving or what is given, under the name of transference, love? And if this gift of speech was the gift of the mother's love, it would give, as to George Sand or to François le Champi, the gift of love as well as the gift of speech.

It is from this perspective that I would read the thematic of the promise (*parole donnée*) in George Sand's work. The promise inaugurates many love stories. Even before being acknowledged as a gift or a bond of love, the gift of a word unites Landry and Fadette or Bernard and Edmée and guarantees their everlasting fidelity. I would say that George Sand conceives of language not as *Verbum* but as *Fides*, as oath (*foi jurée*), binding speech, responsible for repairing the rents of history, which inscribes the subject in the social at the expense of the body. This is why the nuptials, at the end of the rustic narratives, coincide with reunion; the wedding ceremony celebrates the return of the hero who, for a while, has lived in an unfamiliar social scene. It consecrates the victory of the original love bond, the end of separation and its threats, the retaking of the first paths. This last issue is underlined by the Sandian topology of lost paths, paths leading astray or straight to their goal: to the point of departure. In *François le Champi*, *La Petite Fadette* or *La Mare au Diable*, all these paths lead back to the mother.

One can always find one's way back to the mother. Such, too, is the lesson of *Mauprat*. That life offers more than one path, that education can always modify tendencies and allow 'a soul plunged in the depths of an unclean mire as it emerges from the cradle'[27] none the less to develop, illustrates the orientation of this particular apprenticeship: Bernard Mauprat, removed early from the maternal cradle and left to the feudal and masculine barbarity of his uncles, will find in Edmée the educating mother who will help him to unlearn the lessons of his caste, in order to learn how to speak well and to love well.

The direct connection between the maternal tongue and the poetic tongue can be attributed to George Sand's own mother's predispositions. She was the daughter of a bird-seller and a singing bird herself. A 'bird song' that 'his mother Zabelle used to tell him to put him to sleep, in the parlance of the old days of our country'[28] comes to François' mind on his way back to his 'second' 'mother'. Madeleine, whom he has decided to marry.

> Une pive
> cortive,
> Anc ses piviots,
> Cortiviots,
> Livardiots,
> S'en va pivant
> Livardiant
> Cortiviant[29]

It is also in relation to the mother's desire — at least George Sand's mother — that I would interpret the writer's characterization of the road of creation: the path of idealization which she represents as an ascent toward the summit. Here is what she says about it, in a letter to her friend Flaubert, at the moment when she reaches the summit, some months before her death:

As for me I want to gravitate up to my last breath, not with the certitude nor the need of finding elsewhere a good place, but because my sole joy is in keeping myself and mine on an upward road.

In other words *I flee the sewer and I seek the dry and the clean*, certain that it is the law of my existence (added emphasis).[30]

Is not the learning of the dry and the (neat and) clean (*propre*) the paradigm of all first education and the indication of the child's submission to the mother's desire which, in matters of cleanliness, has the force of law? We can confirm this by referring to the scene George Sand describes as a traumatic memory of her early childhood, when her mother snatched her from the pleasure of splashing about in an imaginary river which she called a sewer. We should no longer be surprised by the story George Sand addresses to 'those interested in the making of works of art'[31] in the foreword to *François le Champi*. Here she describes how she took a path 'no one is likely ever to take' which led to a muddy pond she again calls a sewer. Suddenly a wild child sprang over the sewer as if to illustrate Freud's remarks on children's theories of birth. The narrator helped him across the sewer and began to ask him questions, as Madeleine did in the first conversation she had with the Champi, when she found him on the bank of the river. The child, who had no name and no parents, did not know how to answer. George Sand concluded with the necessity for education, recalling that she herself had 'had several Champi of both sexes brought up'.[32]

Does not the law of existence of George Sand's characters consist in having them march in the direction of the dry and the clean (*propre*)? Is not learning to speak well a way of pleasing the mother by sublimating the erotic impulses and displacing them from the anal–genital zone to the mouth? Under the benevolent protection of the first god of George Sand's first religion, Corambé, the mouth tells stories which are so clean the body is nearly absent from them. 'Let's make a novel which would be a religion, or a religion which would be a novel'.[33] Thus was born Corambé, about whom George Sand tells us that she imagined him sometimes with the features of her mother, sometimes with those of a swineherd named Pleasure!

Education, according to George Sand, begins and ends near the river. 'Let's go to the fountain. Maybe I will find my tongue there',[34] François says at the end of the novel. This is where he first met Madeleine, where he was born, so to speak. In the meantime he has learned not to throw himself into the river, not to plunge back into it in a gesture of deadly regression. François and Françoise the Fadette, or even Bernard Mauprat, dirty children of the river, the sewer and the swamp, thus learn, through love, to live, to speak, to wash themselves and to become well behaved (*propres*) — as well behaved and pure as François Rollinat, George Sand's devoted friend, her favourite interlocutor in the rustic novels, the co-singer of a long amebean song, the ultimate addressee of *The Story of My Life*,[35] the representative of an asexual love, the most faithful and perfect of George Sand's life. Indeed George Sand may have taken him for the mother's intermediary: was he not charged with watching over the realization of a desire which had become the law of her existence, the desire transmitted by the mother for a *proper* tongue?[36]

Notes

1. *Histoire de ma vie*, Paris, Gallimard, 1970, Pléiade vol. 1, p. 8. Only certain sections of *The Story of My Life* have been translated. All translations of this and other works cited in this essay are mine unless othe:wise indicated (see note 16).
2. *Histoire de ma vie*, vol. 1 p. 7.
3. 'I must confess that I felt a deathly disgust at imposing my personality on the audience . . . when I felt my heart and my head filled with personalities stronger than myself, more logical, more complete, more ideal, types superior to myself, in a word, characters from a novel.' *Histoire de ma vie*, vol. 1, p. 6.
4. This is the name she gives to this new literary exercise in her preface to *François le Champi*, Paris, Gallimard, 1976, Folio p. 50.
5. *François le Champi*, p. 50.
6. It is still the case today for those who dream not so much of writing as of becoming a writer.
7. George Sand calls it 'bergeries littéraires'.
8. *François le Champi*, p. 52.
9. *François le Champi*, p. 251.
10. *François le Champi*, p. 47.
11. *François le Champi*, p. 52.
12. 'My own style, my phrasing, stood in my way . . . It seemed to me that I daubed the dry, shiny, naive and flat paintings of the primitive masters with oil and tar.' *Jeanne*, Paris, Nelson and Calmann-Levy, p. 8.
13. *Jeanne*, p. 9.
14. See, for instance, *The George Sand–Gustave Flaubert Letters*, translated by Aimée McKenzie, London, Duckworth, 1922.
15. 'When I was only ten years old, my mother left to my care the poor ugly child . . . I cure him when he is ill, whereas my grandmother would kill him, for she does not know how to take care of children; so I preserve this poor little wretch's life . . . And when I think of going out to service, Landry, so as to have some money of my own, and to escape my present poverty, my heart is ready to burst with pity, and accuses me *as if I were my little Grasshopper's mother*, and were letting him die by some fault of mine' (pp. 152–3; added emphasis).

'Landry had listened to little Fadette . . . At last the way in which she spoke of her little brother, the Grasshopper, greatly affected him, and he suddenly felt such a liking for her that he would have defended her against all the world' (*La Petite Fadette* translated by Jane Minot Sedgwick), New York, George H. Richmond, 1893, p. 154.

16. Excerpts from *Histoire de ma vie*, translated and adapted under the title *My Life* by Dan Hofstadter, New York, Harper and Row, 1979, p. 81 (translation modified). For the French see *Histoire de ma vie*, vol. 1, p. 638.
17. *Histoire de ma vie*, vol. 1, p. 15.
18. *Histoire de ma vie*, vol. 1, p. 157.
19. *Histoire de ma vie*, vol. 1, p. 421.
20. *Histoire de ma vie*, vol. 1, p. 76.
21. The narration shifts abruptly from the historical past ('He was sixteen') to an indeterminate present whose generality is emphasized by the use of the indefinite article: 'At that age, *a* boy, raised by *a* tender mother is *an* exceptional being in creation.'
22. *François le Champi*, p. 123.
23. *Histoire de ma vie*, vol. 1, p. 77.
24. *Histoire de ma vie*, vol. 1, p. 77.
25. 'Fonction et champ de la parole et du langage', in *Ecritis*, Seuil, Collection Points, vol. 1, Paris, 1959, p. 159.
26. *Ecrits*, p. 183.
27. *Mauprat*, Paris, Gallimard, 1981, Folio p. 53.
28. *François le Champi*, p. 236.
29. This song of a mother bird and her young is a mixture of Berrichon dialect and literary invention. It is virtually a nonsense rhyme and is untranslatable.
30. *The George Sand–Gustave Flaubert Letters*, 12 January 1876.
31. *François le Champi*, p. 38.
32. *François le Champi*, p. 39.
33. *Histoire de ma vie*, vol. 1, p. 812. Corambé or Corps-en-B (Body-at-B). George Sand recounts that the little Aurore obstinately refused to pronounce the letter 'B' when her mother was teaching her to read, thus resisting the learning of the written code, even when it was taught by her mother, by a single letter. Are we to understand that at 'B' the body escapes linguistic discipline?
34. *François le Champi*, p. 250.
35. She dedicates *The Story of My Life* to him in 1875, 25 years after she completed the book and one year before her death. See the passages of *The Story of My Life* which evoke this relationship, vol. 2, pp. 122–5, p. 758.
36. '*Propre*' means both own (one's own) and clean. Cleanliness is the root of propriety.

5

Crossing the mirror to the forbidden land
(Lewis Carroll's *Alice in Wonderland* and Marina Tsvetaeva's *The Devil*)

Mara Négron Marreo

Translated from the French by Susan Sellers

The texts referred to in this chapter are *Alice's Adventures in Wonderland* and *Through the Looking-glass*. The page references are to *The Complete Works of Lewis Carroll*, London, Nonesuch Press, 1977.
  'The Devil' is Marina Tsvetaeva's account of her own childhood encounters with 'the Devil' and can be found in *A Captive Spirit: Selected Prose*, translated by J. Marin King, London, Virago, 1983. All page references are to this edition.

The imaginary worlds presented in Lewis Carroll's *Alice in Wonderland* and *Through the Looking-glass* and Marina Tsvetaeva's 'The Devil' can be read as a kind of primitive 'forest': the childhood forest to which access normally becomes barred once childhood is left behind. Alice's forest is populated with speaking animals, talking flowers, kings and queens, live cards. Musya's is situated in her sister Valeria's bedroom and comprises a 'devil' who assumes a variety of forms: puns, dreams, cardgames, poems.
  While Valeria and the nurse encourage Musya to go to Valeria's room and look at the books there, Musya's mother considers that she is too young to read and turns Musya's visits into guilty secrets: '(incidentally, she never did come in but only, every single time, at the right moment — as if run on a mechanism — went walking by . . . I would stuff the huge book under the bed' (p. 296). Though Musya is hungry to read she knows that reading is forbidden her; unlike Alice, she is well aware that encountering the forbidden entails guilt as well as pleasure.

In Wonderland, on the contrary, Alice is in the place where hunger is satisfied: Wonderland is a garden of Eden where instead of God's interdict *everything* says 'EAT ME'. In Wonderland everything is back to front: like the reflection in a mirror, the order is reversed. The rabbit-hole can be read as a metaphor for the maternal body, and Alice, instead of coming out from it, returns to the place and time of childhood where oral and bodily relations are predominant, where close bodily contact is the only way of knowing the world. The relation to language is also reversed.

Both Alice and Musya open the door onto another way of knowing. There are books and libraries in both their stories:

> Well, then, the books are something like our books, only the words go the wrong way: I know *that*, because I've held up one of our books to the glass, and then they hold up one in the other room.
>
> (*Through the Looking-glass*, p. 133.)

> Immobilized, I move with my eyes from the empty bed to the fire-bird screen . . . from the screen to the book cabinet, such a strange cabinet where instead of books you see yourself.
>
> ('The Devil', p. 299.)

Thus the library of Looking-glass House can also be found in Tsvetaeva. If there is reflection, it is because there is the mirror. Books with their words reversed reflect the other side of things, of oneself, and so, the other. The reverse is other but the other is also the self reversed: different, other.

In Tsvetaeva's story, the devil is Musya's other. From the way Musya describes it, its sexuality is ambiguous. It possesses both masculine and feminine characteristics:

> There was no fur; there was the opposite of fur: complete smoothness, even clean-shavenness, fresh-cast steeliness. I see now that my devil's body was ideally-athletic: the physique of a female lion, and the colour — of a great Dane.

> There, unmistakably, was — a tail, a lioness's tail, large, bare, strong and vital, like a serpent twisted gracefully in many coils around statuesquely-immobile legs.
>
> (p. 295)

Musya's devil is both lioness and great Dane, both feminine and masculine, and, at the same time, maternal.

Musya is the devil's daughter, joined directly to the devil by an umbilical cord: 'I had my own, direct, inborn tie with the Devil — a direct wire' (p. 308). The devil's main features, however, are its eyes which are 'colourless, passionless and merciless' (p. 296). The knowledge

Musya learns from the devil is thus a way of seeing: a knowledge which perceives of difference without obliterating it, preserving the other. Tsvetaeva's devil is mirror, mother and also placenta-food: the place out of which Musya is born, on the other side of the mirror, to the world of poetry.

> But — maybe it was simpler, maybe it was the poet's inborn passion to juxtapose, to counterpose, and my temperament, the same game that I liked so much to play when I was little: Don't buy black and white, don't say yes and no, only changed around: yes is no, black is white, I am everyone, God is the Devil.
>
> (p. 309)

This exchange between opposites, yes/no, the self/other, God/the Devil, can only take place in the world of poetry. It is the world 'through the looking-glass', where a thing and its image belong together, where difference is included, and where sound and sense shimmer in perpetual play.

Musya's dream about the 'drowned one' is yet another vision of the devil. In her dreams she is carried across the River Oka by a drowned person. Their journey is a voyage across the river of poetry, to the other side of the world, into the space of the imaginary. She dreams of marriage with the drowned one-devil as the conclusion to her search for the 'i' of (the devil's) 'identity' (see p. 298). For, like the crossing through the mirror, this is a journey towards the other and so, towards the self. To answer Alice's question 'who am I?', we have to go through the other. The answer cannot be understood by reason, by exterior forms of knowledge, but has to be felt, from within.

Whereas for Musya the origin of this knowledge is found in Valeria's bedroom, for Alice it is explained in the scene with the Pigeon. The primitive scene of Eden, with the interdiction of its law not to eat the fruit of knowledge, is evoked in the stories in different ways. The Pigeon calls Alice 'serpent' because of her long neck:

> 'I've seen a good many little girls in my time, but never one with such a neck as that! No, no! You're a serpent; and there's no use denying it. I suppose you'll be telling me next that you never tasted an egg!'
>
> 'I have tasted eggs, certainly', said Alice, who was a very truthful child: 'but little girls eat eggs quite as much as serpents do, you know.'
>
> 'I don't believe it', said the Pigeon; 'but if they do, then they're a kind of serpent: that's all I can say.'
>
> (*Alice*, pp. 55–6)

In Tsvetaeva's version the primitive scene is given more explicitly:

But now — I know: the Devil lived in Valeria's room, because in Valeria's room, changed into the shape of the book cabinet, stood the tree of knowledge of good and evil, the fruits of which — Lukhmanova's *Girls*, Staniukovich's *Around the World on the 'Korshun'*, Evgenia Tur's *Catacombs*, *The Bor-Ramensky Family*, and whole years of the magazine *Well-spring* — I so greedily and hastily, guiltily and unrestrainedly gobbled up, keeping an eye out for the door, the way *they* did for God, but without ever betraying *my* serpent. ('Is it Lera who gave you that?' — 'No, I took it myself.') The Devil came into Valeria's room to the place prepared for him: of my transgression — of mother's prohibition.

(p. 300)

Unlike Alice, Musya is fully aware of her transgression. While Alice returns through the mirror to go back again for a second adventure, once Musya has discovered the way through she stays forever. Tsvetaeva's text slips between devil and mother. It is Musya's loss and search for the mother that activates her desire for the forbidden world.

For Musya the guardian of the 'forest' is a god–devil or perhaps a devil–god — Musya is not sure which. Musya's god–devil is very versatile. He takes many forms, especially in games. A game of cards is the setting for the first book of Alice's adventures and Musya is a passionate card-player:

I, at about seven, became impassioned for a while for cards — to a passion. Not for card games — for the cards themselves: all those legless and two-headed, legless and one-armed, but reversed-headed, and reversed-armed, reversed-to-self, turned away from their own selves, at the feet of their own selves and unacquainted with themselves, those highly-placed beings without habitation, but with a whole dependent retinue of like-suited threes and fours.

(p. 303)

from the very first I, who to this day am not secure in the meaning of the gerund and, in general, the significance of grammar, assimilated the meaning of every card: all those roads, money, gossips, news, troubles, matrimonial affairs and official houses — the meaning of a card and what the card ordained.

(p. 304)

The language of the cards is a language which associates numbers, colours, forms. Its meaning flows from this. For Musya it is the language of creation of an imaginary and poetic universe.

The god–devil appears again in Musya's game of Schwarze Peter. The rules of the game consist in getting rid of the Schwarze Peter. Thus the game lies in the gesture. One gives by pretending to take and vice versa.

In order to play you have to know how to give. The more you give the more you have. This giving comes from the inside: 'Maybe I have told about this game too fleshlessly? But what was there in the flesh to tell? You see, there was no action; the whole game was within' (p. 306). It is a game of gestures, a language of gestures originating from the inside. For Musya as for Tsvetaeva this language from within is the origin of the universe: the source of written and spoken knowledge, of poetry: 'It was in me, in me, someone's gift to me in the cradle. 'God-Devil, God-Devil' (p. 308). Like Alice's game of 'let's pretend', it brings Musya in contact with the mirror:

> Setze Du mir einen Spiegel
> Ins Herze hinein . .
>
> I physically felt entering into my breast Valeria's green Venetian mirror in its wreath of tooth-edged crystal, with the gradualness of small teeth: setze-Herze — and the bottomless, middle mirror oval flooding me from shoulder to shoulder and taking me over: Spiegel.
>
> (p. 312)

At the end of Tsvetaeva's story, we find Musya seated next to her mother, her toy devil broken:

> Yes, my devil had burst, not leaving behind either glass or alcohol.
> 'There now, you see', said mother, sitting over my quiet tears, 'you must never become attached to a thing that can break. And they — they all break! Remember the commandment: "Do not make thyself a false idol"?'
>
> (p. 317)

Musya's answer is to ask for a rhyme:

> 'Mama', I said, shaking myself away from tears like a dog from water, 'and what makes rhyme with "idol"? "Adele"?'
>
> (p. 317)

Alice's game of 'let's pretend', Musya's game of 'god–devil' lead both characters back on a journey through the imagination to the forbidden world of childhood: a primitive world that lies beyond the dichotomies of good or evil, where sounds and senses mingle and differences have their place. It is a journey of return to the paradisal world of Eden before the law, to the origin, to the cradle of language out of which poetry is born.

6

Visions of life's tempest: from Shakespeare to Karen Blixen

Nadia Setti

Translated from the French by Susan Sellers

References to 'Tempests' are to the 1986 Penguin edition of *Anecdotes of Destiny*, pp. 71–151; to Peter and Rosa to *Winter's Tales*, Harmondsworth, Penguin, 1983, pp. 146–72.

I want to tell you a story, or, because I am not really a story-teller, but just someone who likes listening to stories, I would like to take you on a reading of a tale by Karen Blixen, alias Isak Dinesen: it is called 'Tempests', a text whose main reference is not a story, but a play — William Shakespeare's *The Tempest*. Like Shakespeare's play Karen Blixen's tale tells a very old story, and we are going to have to cross a great many tempests to get at the heart of the story being told. We can see just by looking at the titles that in moving from the play to the story the tempests have multiplied in number. There are in fact several tempests and each one is the whirlwind moment in the life of someone faced with many possible destinies. We might designate these destinies as: 'woman', 'mother', 'daughter', 'father', 'love', 'death' and so on. The linear succession of these words cannot begin to render the dizzying heights of the tempest which overturns destiny, blurring identities and denominations, and making them unreadable. This 'illisibility' is the condition for our questioning of the world and all its mysteries and for looking differently into the depths of our own being. The tempests reveal truths we thought lost and aspects of ourselves that were until that moment hidden. We can board the tempest as a sort of metaphoric vessel. We might use it to measure the significance of the tempest in Shakespeare and Karen Blixen, though we must none the less expect to be thrown overboard at each stage: for the metaphor to be overturned and for ourselves to be cast out beyond it into the sea.

I am going to consider two of Shakespeare's plays — *King Lear* and *The Tempest* — because of the tempests that rage at their centre and also because Karen Blixen's story presents itself to us as a reading of the plays, a reading which uncovers repressed layers of meaning in Shakespeare and gives them a new development.

Who are the stories' main characters? Thinking of King Lear and his daughters or Prospero and Miranda we might answer: a father and his daughters. But can we really reduce the stories to the father/daughter relationship? Surely such an interpretation reduces the central characters of the plays to falsely rigid roles? I believe we must approach the two stories without knowing in advance who plays who. We must open our ears and listen to the heart of what each character is saying to be able to hear the sense of the words 'father', 'daughter', 'mother', 'woman', 'man': for then the story might begin to tell itself differently.

In the opening scene of Act 1, King Lear reveals his decision to share his kingdom between his three daughters. The division will take place on condition of each of his daughters replying to a demand:

Tell me, my daughters,
(Since now we will divest us both of rule,
Interest of territory, cares of state)
Which of you shall we say doth love us most?

(Act 1, Scene 1, lines 50–3.)

What is so surprising and misleading about this opening scene is that King Lear does not just ask a question: he makes a total demand of his daughters. He forces them to outdo each other in their declarations of love for him, to be the 'more-than-daughters' of a 'more-than-father', as if, towards the end of his life, he wants to capitalize on Love. And in her reply, each daughter reveals her 'filial' substance. Regan and Goneril throw themselves into carrying out their father's request according to the rules, offering Lear the mirror of Love he requires, whereas when Cordelia (who has been in the 'asides' of the official discourse right from the start) is asked to speak she offers no words which mirror, no flattering image but utters just one word. A word which cleaves both the discourse and the request: 'nothing'. Lear has been expecting everything and she says 'nothing'. Cordelia's refusal blinds Lear: suddenly Lear can no longer see himself, it is as if just one word, a 'nothing', has taken away the mask and left him with the image of, precisely — nothing. For the time being Lear remains deaf to the full significance of this 'nothing' which, if he could hear it, would dismantle his royal narcissism; but it is this 'nothing' which will implant itself in Lear's heart and give rise to the tempest.

Lear is used to the flattery of self-love; what Cordelia tries so dangerously to offer him is the love of . . . Cordelia, that is: 'nothing'.

Lear had thought to live out the last of his days with Cordelia but her words force him to measure himself with destiny, to cast off all the false discourses which have sustained him, and finally face 'the thing itself': death, without a mask. This is the real meaning of the division of the kingdoms: nothing more nor less than the sharing out of paths and destinies, which lead Cordelia out of her father's house and into the world and Lear to confront his own mortality.

For this is the final lesson of this 'nothing'. Lear has to lose everything: his kingdom, his royal mask, his daughters, even his mind, in order to be able to learn the quality of true love and the mortal value of life. When, in the fifth act, Lear and Cordelia finally come together, they are no longer the 'father' and the 'daughter' of the opening scene. Instead they are beings who have undergone death and bereavement, they have crossed through the tempests of destiny and history. The tempest strips away Lear's blindness engendering Cordelia's rebirth in his heart, as well as his own birth, not as royal Lear but, simply, a 'man'. In the final analysis Lear and Cordelia are both children of the storm.

We have crossed the tempest of *King Lear* to arrive at the shore of *The Tempest*. *The Tempest* is the last of Shakespeare's plays and marks the birth of the new era which neither Lear nor Cordelia lived to see. While *King Lear* is the story of loss and laying bare, in *The Tempest* loss is transformed. Prospero has lost a kingdom but with the aid of his magic power he creates a new kingdom on the island. *The Tempest* is a play about the dreams that rework and play upon reality. Crossing the tempest we come on the other side of death to a magic place where dreams and reality are no longer clearly distinguishable from each other. And as is often the case in dreams, what is shown on the dream island of *The Tempest* is the hidden truth of reality.

Prospero displays his art for the benefit of his young daughter Miranda. At the beginning of the play Miranda is still the child who has not yet been confronted with the experience of separation, loss and death. Her knowledge of the world is confined to Prospero and the beings who inhabit the island. But the experience of loss comes almost immediately. In the opening scene of the play a tempest explodes. The result of this tempest is that right up until the end there are a number of characters who believe that they are lost and that those they were with died in the storm. However, since none of the characters actually die in the storm, their experience of loss is not founded in a real loss but in an imaginary one. Nevertheless, for the play's protagonists this distinction is blurred. What matters is that the characters confront death: they come up against the fact of their own mortality as well as the possibility of others' death. On the one hand there are those characters who are led astray by the storm, on the other stands Prospero, the person responsible for unleashing the tempest. By the end of the play all the characters will know what it is to have lost, they will have undergone the experience of losing but they will have come out of the experience alive, to rediscover themselves on the other shore.

I said that the tempest marked Cordelia's rebirth in Lear's heart and the tempest unleashed by Prospero brings about the new birth of Miranda. Through the tempest Miranda experiences suffering for the first time. She witnesses the fate of the ship-wrecked sailors: 'O, I have suffered/With those that I saw suffer . . . . O, the cry did knock/Against my very heart! Poor souls, they perished' (Act 1, Scene 2, lines 5–9). The sailors' suffering opens a window on the world for Miranda, on to the tempest-torn sea where life is in constant struggle against death. Now Miranda is ready to listen to Prospero's account of his former life and of how he was forced to flee his kingdom on pain of death. Her acknowledgement of loss enables her to leave the world of childhood behind her and to assume her adult identity as 'no wonder . . . but certainly a maid' (Act 1, scene 2, lines 424–5) — no longer a child of dreams but a young girl in person and in fact.

In order to remain alive Cordelia had to shape a word — her exit — as a means of asserting herself against the threat of her obliteration. But Miranda is not Cordelia. As a result of the tempest Miranda, unlike Cordelia, is forced to confront reality and not just the threat of death.

Nor is Prospero King Lear. Prospero can bring about sleep, waking, dreams: the all-mighty power of the magician can transform dreams into reality. Together with Ariel he makes up a unit resembling that of the Ego and the Id, for like the Ego he is constantly in the process of channelling and structuring the disobedient, flitting pulsions of the Id. For Miranda he acts as the reality principle, leading her towards the discovery of the other beyond their harmonious duet of the island-world. Unlike Lear he creates the necessary conditions that include a tempest to bring about the transition from love for himself, the father, to love for Ferdinand.

Is Prospero's role that of the 'father'? or the 'mother'? On the world of the island roles and genders are not fixed: they are symbolized by Ariel, a spirit of the air, who can literally take any form he chooses, as well as by those who arrive on the island as a result of the tempest and who are thrown so far off course that most will never be the same again.

The overwhelming effects of the tempest have a profound influence on all the play's characters, who live for a while after it in a state of transition. The tempest overturns the barrier between conscious and unconscious, blurring identities and distinctions and bringing to the surface the repressed elements of existence that form the truth of our human mortality.

So let us imagine that these stories continue on their voyage across the seas and through time to Denmark, where Karen Blixen is waiting to receive and re-tell them.

Karen Blixen has transplanted the island of *The Tempest* into a theatre belonging to a Herr Soerensen who is to put on Shakespeare's play. Already the characters of Karen Blixen's tale have a double life: the life they lead on Soerensen's stage and the one they lead in reality. This is particularly true of the character who is called Malli in real life and Ariel on stage, and who is the meeting point for all the characters and tempests in the story.

Herr Soerensen is a dreamer, the character to whom Karen Blixen will attribute her own dreams and inner landscape: a foreign landscape which is both beyond and greater than the self: 'He had kept a deep, undying passion for the land of fells, which in his mind loomed heaven-aspiring and wind-swept' (p. 71). These are the visions of a young adolescent standing on the brink of life. They are Peter's visions from Karen Blixen's story 'Peter and Rosa': the desire for distance, for remoteness, the deep-felt desire for release from the earth and from all those who are rooted there — for birth and death in the seas and in the sky:

> Higher up, in the lofts of the world, perhaps big swarms of quails, thrushes and snipes were on the move. Such a tremendous stream of longing, on its way to its goal, passed above his head, that Peter, down on the ground, felt his limbs ache. He flew a long way with the geese.
>
> ('Peter and Rosa', p. 147)

The sky is the inverted image of the sea; the sea is another sky to which Peter's body belongs.

> The deep-water currents would pass through his eyes, like a row of clear, green dreams — big fish, whales even, would float above him like clouds, and a shoal of small fishes might suddenly rush along, an endless streak, like the birds tonight.
>
> ('Peter and Rosa', p. 147)

Herr Soerensen retains these childhood visions which provide the inspiration for his vision on stage. He uproots himself from his native soil to implant himself in the theatre. It is this visionary earth — 'the vision of the tempest' — that gives birth to the young girl, Malli, who will play Ariel. Herr Soerensen makes his choice irrespective of sexual identity. He has his own ideas about sexual difference, believing that 'woman is to man what poetry is to prose, then are the womenfolk we come across from day to day poems read aloud' (p. 76). By giving this role to a girl Karen Blixen emphasizes Ariel's sexual ambiguity: both girl and boy s/he is a creature caught on the wing, a young person whose body is in the process of transformation.

Once Malli has been assigned her stage role, the narrative retraces her story back to the time of her birth, showing us the path that has led her to the stage. A 'child of love' (p. 78), she is both a mother's daughter and daughter of the sea where her missing father lies.

The first tempest of the story breaks out when Malli's desire to be Ariel comes up against her mother's desire to keep a hold on her. There is a third protagonist in this struggle: the lover-father, the absent ever-present figure around whose ghost the tempest between the two women rages. The tempest arises out of the father's memory, out of the very depths of love, and the struggle between mother and daughter climaxes in a love-battle as the mother comes to recognize in her daughter the image of her lost lover.

This return of the ghost of love is not so much Malli's father as the representative of everything Madame Ross 'doesn't understand': 'Now, whether in punishment or reward, through all eternity she must love and believe in what she did not understand' (p. 85). The missing father thus becomes a sort of posthumous divinity: linked to the force of the tempest he represents the ambivalent power of both life and death, passion as well as madness, the journey through the imaginary as well as the inevitable force of reality. All these elements are stages which will constitute Malli's apprenticeship to life.

The return of the repressed ghost of the father coincides in the text with the pronouncement of Malli's name. Malli's mother gave her daughter the name of the heroine of a song sung by Malli's father. 'Malli' is also a name which has associations with Malli's grandmother: thus for Malli's mother, 'Malli' represents her lover's mother as well as her lover. The complexity of identities is present on both sides: both the mother and daughter are carried to the outer edges of the self, to the point where identities dissolve and are lost. They are thus brought to the brink of the farewell scene in which the daughter re-presents the living figure of the father to the mother and the battle is transformed into a new union.

> During the time in which she strove against her daughter's obsession she inexplicably lived her short marriage over again. It was from day to day the same surprises and emotions: a foreign, rich and enrapturing power, that had once taken her by storm, again surrounded her on all sides . . . She fell in love with her daughter as she had once fallen in love with the father, so that . . . when finally in a stormy and tearful interview she gave the girl her blessing, it was to her as if she were being wed again.
>
> (p. 85)

We might ask, where does this blessing come from? Is it the mother's blessing, or the blessing of love which arises out of the mother's love for the lost lover-father as he is resurrected in the daughter? In the final necessary act of separation, it is love for the father which blesses the union between mother and daughter; the point at which the love of the mistress-wife for the lover and mother for the daughter meet. Since this love is born under the sign of separation it is also the point at which the mother and father, atoned for here with the additional element of father's destiny.

The father's disappearance weighs in the story from the beginning. It acts as a suspended point of severance: we do not know whether the father is really dead or whether he simply did not return. This also explains why judgement on the father is suspended (did he or did he not abandon Malli's mother?) and why Malli has thus been able to create for herself the imaginary figure of a heroic father.

The struggle between mother and daughter ending in union redresses the act of suspension. The initial separation is re-lived giving rise to the scene which never took place: the final farewell scene between Malli's mother and father, atoned for here with the additional element of benediction.

The union also consecrates Malli's relationship with the father's ghost, leading Malli towards Ariel, child of the air, capable of conjuring tempests and resurrecting the dead. In her role as Ariel, Malli is pupil to the father-magician Prospero. The aerial quality of the character she plays casts her as a fluid, multiple identity, while in Prospero (Herr Soerensen) she discovers a fictitious father-figure whose symbolic image is magically insured against loss.

Just when the stage would seem to be set for the enactment of Soerensen's production of *The Tempest* a real tempest explodes. This time it is no stage drama which takes place but a storm off the coast of Norway. The tempest interrupts the play's progress and is marked by a change of register in the narrative; the raging of this storm is recounted in an article in a newspaper which is both detached from and outside the world of the play. We move from one fiction to another: the first part of the story unfolds the characters' visions of tempest whilst the second part involves a shift in narrative transposing the characters to a new and different reality. The thrust of this reality will become an increasingly important element in the resolution of the story.

We immediately realize that the Norwegian tempest has given birth to another Malli, for Malli is now seen as a heroine, as someone who has returned alive from the dead. If before she had represented the (lost) father's love to the mother she is now also hailed as the redeemer of loss, as the person responsible for saving the lives of those on board the 'Sofie Hosenwinckel'. In fact Malli is reborn on several counts: as a heroine, as a saving 'angel' and as the young girl gathered from the sea by the fairy-tale 'prince' Arndt Hosenwinckel.

The rapid series of events that follow the tempest are written under the sign of inversion. Just as Malli and Arndt decide to become engaged like characters in a real fairy story the tempest breaks out again. Ferdinand, the young sailor who had stood at Malli's side on the helm of the 'Sofie Hosenwinckel' throughout the tempest, suddenly dies. For the first time Malli is brought face to face with the actual fact of death. Here it is no longer the living ghost of an imaginary death which confronts her but the reality of a dead body.

As in any process of mourning Malli begins by interiorizing death. She merges with her image of the dead Ferdinand to the point at which she comes to physically resemble his corpse. Her attempt at bodily substitution is emphasized by a change she makes to the original text of Ariel's song:

> Full fathom five my body lies,
> Of my bones are coral made,
> Those are pearls that were my eyes,
> Nothing of me that doth fade,
> But doth suffer a sea-change
> Into something rich and strange.
> Sea-nymphs hourly ring my knell.
> Hark! Now I hear them — ding dong bell.
>   (p. 144, cf *The Tempest*, Act 1, scene 2, lines 394–400).

Whereas in Shakespeare's text it is 'thy father's' body that lies at the bottom of the sea, in Malli's song it is '*my* body' which is transformed and exchanged in the depths: it is not just 'thy father' who dies but also 'myself'. There is substitution but also several levels of transformation. There is transformation of Shakespeare's text, transformation of one body into another, and transformation of these bodies into 'something rich and strange'; magic words, a song, hidden treasure.

It is important to remember the circumstances in which the song is sung. Malli sings as she returns to ask Herr Soerensen for his advice. After Ferdinand's death and her own death by substitution she is no longer the same Ariel who ran at Prospero's side but a mortal angel fallen to earth. As a result of her visit Herr Soerensen resumes the role of the character who through his art survives death: he is not King Lear and neither is Malli to be identified with Cordelia.

> He at first felt that their group was taking form like that of the old unhappy king and his loving daughter. But presently the centre of gravity was shifted and he became fully conscious of his authority and responsibility: he was no fugitive, it was his young disciple who

had fled to him for help. He once more became the man powerful above others: Prospero.

(p. 141)

Herr Soerensen–Prospero offers Malli a stable point of anchorage, the solid earth of *The Tempest*-island from which she can return to the world. And he gives her his blessing for the new life waiting for her in the words which release Ariel in Shakespeare's play: 'My Ariel, chick, then to the elements be free and fare thou well!' (p. 145).

But before she can be released Malli must in turn free Arndt from their engagement. She writes him a farewell letter, a letter which draws into it her father's unwritten letter of farewell to her mother. It is thus a letter of separation which atones for loss, reversing its meaning and effect in the rediscovery of the value of love. In her letter Malli recounts her experience of the storm, describing to Arndt how she did not live through it as Malli but as Ariel, spirit of the air, incorporeal, and therefore outside the spheres of death and fear. But Ferdinand's death brought her back to the reality of the human tempest, in which she realizes that their dream of love can have no place. In offering Arndt this letter, Malli offers him the gift of her vision, a gift which is not without its price since it involves both of them in the renunciation of happiness. For the gift means the irredeemable loss of the fairy-tale world where she and Arndt could have lived together forever sheltered from life's tempests.

Malli concludes her letter to Arndt by telling him that if another tempest breaks out she will live through it differently.

I may again run into such a storm as the one in Kvasefjord. But that this time I shall clearly understand that it is not a play in the theatre but it is death. And it seems to me that then, in the last moment before we go down, I can in all truth be yours. And I am thinking that it will be fine and great to let wave-beat cover heart-beat. And in that hour to say: 'I have been saved, because I have met you and looked at you, Arndt!'

(p. 151)

What Malli has learned as a result of the tempest is the price that has to be paid for reality. She realizes that she can no longer pass between dream and reality as she could in her role as Ariel; that only death has the power to make the love she dreams of definitive. Her vision of the inescapable fact of the human condition forces her to abandon this dream of a sheltered love, inviting Arndt in its stead to an uncertain union with the tempestuous reality of living.

As she writes this last letter to Arndt, Malli composes her first poem which is like a nursery rhyme.

> I have made you poor, my sweetheart dear.
> I am far from you when I am near.
> I have made you rich, my dearest heart.
> I am near when we are far apart.

(p. 149)

One of the first things that strikes us is the repetition of the 'I' which opens each line of verse. Like the I which inscribes itself in the letter, the I of the verse is the subject which leaves and thus causes separation, but which also holds out the possibility of redress. 'Rich' and 'poor', 'near' and 'far' are two sides of the same coin: Arndt is 'poor' because deprived of Malli's presence but this same absence may be transformed into wealth through the vision Malli offers. Malli inherited her father's absence in the gold coin he left her mother, and she gives this coin to Arndt as she confides the secret of her vision in her letter. This gold coin, which circulates from one hand to the other (and the hands which give instantly disappear in the passing), is thus symbolically charged, recalling loss as well as those who are lost, the redemption of loss as well as the price of access to life.

7

Djuna Barnes' *Nightwood*: where man is with wo(e)

Mairéad Hanrahan

Page references are first to the UK edition of *Nightwood* (London, Faber and Faber, 1936) and are followed by reference to the US edition (New York, New Directions, 1946).

Djuna Barnes' *Nightwood* is a tale of misery: a tale of misery told in misery, a misery deemed the inescapable, even the only identifiable, characteristic of the 'human condition'. Indeed, *Nightwood* is no other than a torturous questioning of what, for Djuna Barnes, the 'human condition' may be. Torturous, and tortured: a key to the writing of the book is to be found early on when Nora tells Felix and the doctor that they 'argue about sorrow and confusion too easily' (p. 39/21); these subjects would rather require a long and painfully involved elaboration. Exactly such an elaboration is *Nightwood*.

The novel indeed revolves around painful involvement, involvement in the sense of an agonized participation in life (sorrow) as well as in that of a circuitous and radical impossibility to be simple (confusion). Sorrow and confusion are to be encountered at every level of this book (characters, author, language, etc.); they are linked inevitably with being alive, with the search for a form which being alive entails. Thus the importance of the frequent recurrence of the word 'predicament': being human is a predicament, a painful ('sticky') situation where no turning or particular direction is indicated, where no outlet is possible.

The very first paragraph of *Nightwood* signals that life is regrettable from the outset: the suspicion is 'well-founded' 'as to the advisability of perpetuating that race which has the sanction of the Lord and the disapproval of the people' (p. 11/1). Not, of course, that this inadvisability is limited to any particular race (the Jews); more than anyone else, the Catholic Irishman (from America), Dr O'Connor, whose long, rambling, desperately impassioned speeches give the book so much of its atmosphere of naked pain, expresses the conviction that life is anguish, a

time of fruitless struggling against mortality, an extended death-rattle
shared by all; as, for example, when Nora is learning that pain is
inconsolable.

> Isn't everyone in the world peculiarly swung and me the craziest of
> the lot? — so that I come dragging and squealing, like a heifer on
> the way to slaughter, knowing his cries have only half a rod to go,
> protesting his death — as his death has only a rod to go to protest
> his screaming? Do you walk high Heaven without shoes? Are you
> the only person with a bare foot pressed down on a rake?
>
> (p. 218/155)

Even the most desperate anguish serves no end: he cries elsewhere that
'Rage and inaccuracy howl and blow the bone, for, contrary to all
opinion, all suffering does *not* purify' (p. 196/138). His only advice is, in
effect, to want nothing, to have no aspiration to wrench form from
chaos:

> Be humble like the dust, as God intended, and crawl, and finally
> you'll crawl to the end of the gutter and not be missed and not
> much remembered.
>
> (p. 208/147)

Only by accepting one's mortality, by not seeking any relief (in all senses)
from formlessness, can one attain an 'end': death is the only 'end'. His
advice therefore is not a remedy: if the only relief from life is death, life
must be irremediably painful since being alive, as we shall now see for
the characters in *Nightwood*, means having a passionate desire for an
impossible 'end'. Their desperate passion for extremity is alone extreme.

Felix, the Baron, for example leads a desperate search for a character,
an identity, some feature to distinguish him. He is in total confusion, in
need of a destiny:

> wishing to be correct at any moment, he was tailored in part for the
> evening and in part for the day.
> From the mingled passions that made up his past, out of a diversity
> of bloods, from the crux of a thousand impossible situations, Felix
> had become the accumulated and single — the embarrassed.
>
> (p. 21/8)

Incapable of concentration or specialization, unable to do anything
requiring selection on his part, Felix is wholly inappropriate; he is
'embarrassed' in the sense of 'jumbled together' as well as of not
knowing what, or even whether, to say or do ('In restaurants he bowed
slightly to anyone who looked as if he might be "someone", making the
bend so imperceptible that the surprised person might think he was

merely adjusting his stomach' (p. 22/9). A mess, a mass, both single and embarrassed, he cannot participate in anything.

Thus, unable to create an identity for himself, he hopes to attain one from outside; by adopting a (false) title he hopes that aristocracy might provide the means to an 'end' and enable his line to end in distinction. (With his son it does, but in a bitterly ironic way. Felix' son, Guido, does have a life which is 'peculiarly [his] own' (p. 169/118), i.e., which belongs to him, therefore he does attain an 'end'; but it is that of idiocy. With his son Felix achieves a certain distinction but only that of degradation; as the doctor predicts when Felix confides his hopes for a son to him: 'we go up — but we come down' (p. 63/40).) Furthermore, the world of titles he enters is the 'pageantry of the circus and the theatre', the world of representation, thus of false identities; the only whole of which he is a part is itself a 'splendid and reeking falsification'. Nor is he distinctive even in this: 'The people of this world, with desires utterly divergent from his own, had also seized on titles for a purpose' (p. 25/11). For them, too, nobility is a means to an illusory end — his desire is only one of many. The title of Baron merely masks the distance between him and his desires. 'Felix clung to his title to dazzle his own estrangement. It brought them together'. It cannot transform his fundamental inappropriateness.

Both accumulated and single, he is neither a whole (because he has no parts, nothing can be singled out in him), nor a part of any greater whole (he can only 'dazzle' his 'estrangement', participate in 'falsification'). Yet this condition of confusion is part of being human — Barnes would seem to be saying that we are all alone in being lonely. Nowhere is this more evident than in the passage of magnificent writing introducing Frau Mann, whose name immediately and explicitly inscribes a confusion of the sexes.

> It was to the Duchess of Broadback (Frau Mann) that Felix owed his first audience with a 'gentleman of quality.' Frau Mann, then in Berlin, explained that this person had been 'somewhat mixed up with her in the past.' It was with the utmost difficulty that he could imagine her 'mixed up' with anyone, her coquetries were muscular and localized. Her trade — the trapeze — seemed to have preserved her. It gave her, in a way, a certain charm. Her legs had the specialized tension common to aerial workers; something of the bar was in her wrists, the tan bark in her walk, as if the air, by its very lightness, by its very non-resistance, were an almost insurmountable problem, making her body, though slight and compact, seem much heavier than that of women who stay upon the ground. In her face was the tense expression of an organism surviving in an alien element. She seemed to have a skin that was the pattern of her

costume: a bodice of lozenges, red and yellow, low in the back and
ruffled over and under the arms, faded with the reek of her three-a-
day control, red tights, laced boots — one somehow felt they ran
through her as the design runs through hard holiday candies, and
the bulge in the groin where she took the bar, one foot caught in
the flex of the calf, was as solid, specialized and as polished as oak.
The stuff of the tights was no longer a covering, it was herself; the
span of the tightly stitched crotch was so much her own flesh that
she was as unsexed as a doll. The needle that had made one the
property of the child made the other the property of no man.

(p. 26/12)

This is not the place to attempt to unravel the skeins of this inexhaustible
passage; we shall merely try to follow the movement of the text in the
description of her properties.

The first sentence opens on an uncertain axis. In order to go *up* on the
social scale (meet a 'gentleman of quality'), Felix needs the Duchess of
Broadback, a name which evokes the horizontal axis, and even, crudely,
a broad on her back. She is, furthermore, a trapeze-artist. Thus going *up*
entails going *across*, 'quality' is associated with vulgarity, the one
inextricable from the other. The text is then displaced towards the
explicit discussion of entanglement and we read that she who least seems
'mixed up' with anyone (because 'localized', fixed in one place) is 'mixed
up' with this gentleman. Her apparent specificity or definiteness seems
the result of her trade — but already the definiteness is showing itself to
be representation, therefore illusion: 'Her trade *seemed* to have preserved
her. It gave her, *in a way*, a certain charm.' In the next sentence, it is
progressively undermined: the 'specialized' tension is 'common' to aerial
workers — the sentence endows her with a particularity only to take it
away; 'something of the bar' is already less specific and the sentence ends
with a simile ('as if the air . . .'; a simile, moreover, associating the
opposites of lightness and heaviness in an image whose very form seems
to dissolve into the words composing it; a whole seemingly shown by its
crumbling to be no more than the sum of its parts), that is, in the realm of
illusion: the illusion of a further illusion ('making her body *seem* much
heavier').

Her trade may endow her with at least the appearance of certain
characteristics but she must struggle constantly to maintain the illusion
or it will reveal itself for what it is; and as with Frau Mann, so with the
text. 'In her face was the tense expression of an organism surviving in an
alien element.' For these properties to endure, she must wholly adopt
their design; not only her skin but the entire thickness of her body takes
the appearance of her costume; the difference between surface and depth
is blurred, and everything is given over to — becomes a means for —

illusion. This powerful sentence ends with her sex not in flux, indeterminate, but rather solid, shaped, determinate ('and the bulge in the groin where she took the bar, one foot caught in the flex of the calf, was as solid, specialized and as polished as oak'). Total commitment to her art enables her sex to assume an appearance — the appearance of no sex (she is 'as unsexed as a doll'). The trapeze affords her an identity, the only identity possible in her confusion: that of no sexual identity. She is in a sexual 'no man's land', neither man nor woman. And at this point the text reverts to the categorical, and 'was' replaces 'seems', four times inscribed in the one sentence. 'The stuff of the tights was no longer a covering, it was herself; the span of the tightly stitched crotch was so much her own flesh that she was as unsexed as a doll.'

The trapeze could be read as a metaphor for writing and, as Frau Mann becomes 'herself', gains a 'herself' through the abdication of her body to her art, so Djuna Barnes hopes to gain some 'property', some identity, even if it must be that of no sexual identity. For the only property possible is the 'property of no man': like Felix, by embracing a title (that of an artist), she can only hope to 'dazzle her estrangement'. The fundamental condition of sexual indeterminacy cannot be altered; an illusion, no matter how wholeheartedly adopted, remains an illusion. Frau Mann (to whom we shall later return) remains confused.

Confusion is the lot of all of *Nightwood*'s characters. Nora Flood, as her name suggests, experiences it most absolutely.

> Her house was couched in the centre of a mass of tangled grass and weeds. Before it fell into Nora's hands the property had been in the same family two hundred years.
>
> (p. 77/50)

Nora's property has 'fallen' into her hands, has suffered degradation — to the point of being the 'paupers' salon, receiving people without property (the doctor at one point says that paupers are 'impersonal with misery'). She lives in flux, in a world devoid of solidity, a world which has lost its definiteness.

Yet at first she does not suffer from this condition.

> There is a gap in 'world pain' through which the singular falls continually and forever; a body falling in observable space, deprived of the privacy of disappearance; as if privacy, moving relentlessly away, by the very sustaining power of its withdrawal kept the body eternally moving downward, but in one place, and perpetually before the eye. Such a singular was Nora.
>
> (p. 79/51)

Though like all the other characters in that she is 'descending', going down, suffering a fall, Nora is unaware of the pain of this 'human

condition' of perpetual degradation and loss. She is oblivious to the
world about her, which joins in her disappropriation ('Nora robbed
herself for everyone, incapable of giving herself warning, she was
continually turning about to find herself diminished' (p. 79/51)); yet even
without her 'wits' about her, it is nevertheless she who most bears
witness to that world, in the degradation of her property.

> Those who love everything are despised by everything, as those
> who love a city, in its profoundest sense, become the shame of that
> city, the *détraqués*, the paupers; *their good is incommunicable, outwitted,*
> *being the rudiment of a life that has developed, as in man's body are found*
> *evidences of lost needs.* This condition had struck even into Nora's
> house; it spoke in her guests, in her ruined gardens where she had
> been wax in every work of nature.
>
> (p. 80/52; added emphasis)

It is precisely Nora's lack of characteristics (her degraded property)
which most preserves what has been lost (and which Nora loves, unaware
that she can never regain it); or alternatively, the past can persist only
because Nora does not (cannot) appropriate an identity for herself; its
preservation depends on her desire being unsatisfied. But at the start she
is not yet conscious of the craving within her for this 'lost' property.

> The world and its history were to Nora like a ship in a bottle; she
> herself was outside and unidentified, endlessly embroiled in a
> preoccupation without a problem.
>
> (p. 82/53)

Propertyless, Nora carries the world, the past within her. No suffering
afflicts her because her desire is not awakened — her preoccupation
(absentmindedness, also pre-occupation: a period before she occupies, a
period before she asserts herself as subject) is not a problem.

But then: 'Then she met Robin'. And Robin activates the longing of
which Nora had lived oblivious, and with her love — necessarily,
according to the logic of this book, because of her love — Nora meets
with suffering, a suffering all the more overwhelming in that it takes her
unawares.

Robin seems superficially the negative of Nora: whereas the latter
seemed at first to be all inside, to have no surface, Robin apparently is
only surface. While Nora loves everybody, Robin loves nobody. She
seems content as an object, indeed her attraction for the other characters
lies in her quality of absence, her extreme unassertiveness; as if these
were the attributes of a plenitude leaving nothing to be desired. The
evening in Jenny's house, Robin is said to be the only person to have
'come to the end of her existence' (p. 105/10). She is presented as 'a
"picture" forever arranged (p. 59/37), that is, as an image stabilized in

the flux in time. Her attraction is that of an image, the attraction of an object which has no desire of its own and on to which we can project (thus give an apparent materiality to) our desire for an unchangeable, unchanging world, a time before history — that is, eternity.

> Such a woman is the infected carrier of the past: before her the structure of our head and jaws ache — we feel that we could eat her, she who is eaten death returning, for only then do we put our face close to the blood on the lips of our forefathers.
>
> (p. 60/37)

She offers the possibility of unicity, an image of death in life; in her confusion seems untroubled by desire: 'as if this girl were the converging halves of a broken fate, setting face, in sleep, toward itself in time' (p. 60/38).

Barnes insists throughout the book on Robin's androgynous appearance; she is taller than the average woman, 'a tall girl with the body of a boy', dressed in 'boys' clothes' ('white flannel trousers'), with 'feet large and as earthly as the feet of a monk' (that is, of a celibate man). Nor is her name a clear indication of the sex she belongs to. This 'middle condition' between the sexes is for the doctor the source of her fascination; it is responsible for the 'slovenliness that is usually an accompaniment of the "attractive" body, a sort of earth on which love feeds' (p. 169/118). This middle condition' does not inspire in her a desire for extremity, for order, for form. ('Destiny and history are untidy; we fear memory of that disorder. Robin did not.' (p. 169/118).) The Baron concurs:

> This quality of *one sole condition*, which was so much a part of the Baronin, was what drew me to her; a condition of being that she had not, at that time, even chosen, but a *fluid sort of possession*.
>
> (p. 161/112; added emphasis)

Robin would thus appear to be herself in being nobody, her property (possession) is having none, being in flux (fluid); she does not object to being *wholly confused*. Hers is the charm of the 'invert', 'boy or girl' — a charm to which the doctor, himself equally in confusion as we shall see, is especially sensible:

> We were impaled in our childhood upon them as they rode through our primers, the sweetest lie of all, now come to be in boy or girl, for in the girl it is the prince, and in the boy it is the girl that makes a prince a prince — and not a man. They go far back in our lost distance where what we never had stands waiting; it was inevitable that we should come upon them, for our miscalculated longing has created them.
>
> (p. 194/136)

Thus it is that Robin is the object of desire of men and women alike: in her apparent asexuality (she is like a prince and a monk, a boy, that is an unformed man), she represents a lost paradise of completude, a paradise which nobody alive has ever enjoyed ('where what we never had stands waiting'); she represents death. Nora comes to realize this; she cries: 'Love is death, come upon with passion' (p. 195/13). Her suffering is unmitigated because, being totally unprepared for what she will feel for Robin, she abandons herself entirely to her passion before understanding that her love (all love, in Djuna Barnes' eyes) is necessarily hopeless: it is the desire for the impossible, it is being condemned in life to long for death. In her words 'Everything we can't bear in this world, some day we find in one person, and love it all at once' (p. 192/135). What we love is what we cannot tolerate, but also what we cannot carry ourselves, everything we have had to let go, to *not* have, in our struggle to be a person. We love only what we cannot have, 'in this world', we love only death.

Yet Robin offers only the representation of death. Nobody alive is free from desire; nobody can choose to want nothing. Robin too is human and keeping the sorrow of the human condition at a distance depends on her seeking no security, on her refusing all participation. For if, as the doctor declares, 'Man has no foothold that is not also a bargain' (p. 53/32), then the search for certainty or identity leads to compromise, shattering the illusion of completude and inaugurating desire for what has been conceded.

Robin's safety from anguish therefore rests on a terrible sort of purity, in which the morality of her actions is beyond question, as if somehow she were not present to assume them.

> She prayed, and her prayer was monstrous because in it there was no margin left for damnation or forgiveness, for praise or for blame — those who cannot conceive a bargain cannot be saved or damned. She could not offer herself up; she only told of herself in a *preoccupation* that was its own *predicament*.
>
> (p. 72/47; added emphasis)

Two key words we have already encountered reappear, this time in relation to each other. Her preoccupation is its own predicament: her thoughts are 'unpeopled', as Barnes specifies elsewhere, as though no subject arranges them; their chaos is at once a problem to be kept at a distance and a prediction. Robin is a subject only through 'preoccupation', that is, by not predicating herself, by not assuming the status of subject. Robin's identity is predicated on having no identity.

Yet even the immense passivity she nourishes is not sufficient to save her from suffering — she is forced into contact with the world outside herself. She bears a son to Felix:

A week out of bed she was lost, as if she had done something irreparable, as if this act had caught her attention for the first time.
(p. 74/48)

She flees in horror away from this first contact, this first home calling for her participation, in a desperate attempt to regain her disturbed somnolence. She meets Nora and sets up house with her; from now on she is torn between 'two spirits', 'love and anonymity' — for the first time she expresses a 'wish for a home'. She too desires. Her life will be an endless cycle of comings and goings — she leaves Nora for Jenny and Jenny also will discover that Robin cannot bear attachment. Robin can no longer totally absent herself from living; in her are mingled the need to be loved (for example, she needs Nora's faith in her, p. 199/140) and the need not to love ('Every bed she leaves, without caring, fills her heart with peace and happiness' (p. 207/146)), the need to be remembered and the need to forget — always together, neither ever adequate. She is condemned to an eternal conflict between her awakened desire for an identity, a form given to her by someone else, and her longing for her previous oblivion where she had wanted nothing. Robin, like all of Djuna Barnes' world, finds that confusion is not separable from sorrow.

If even Robin learns the Barnesian lesson that life is confusion and sorrow, there is little chance that Jenny should not suffer the consequences of her voracious appetite for an identity, so viciously portrayed in the first four pages of the chapter 'The squatter'. Everything about her is inappropriate: her head and body 'did not go together', she is 'unable to wear anything becoming'. Totally devoid of a sense of herself, she appropriates anything of importance to someone else.

Her walls, her cupboards, her bureaux, were teeming with second-hand dealings with life. It takes a bold and authentic robber to get first-hand plunder. Someone else's marriage ring was on her finger; the photograph taken of Robin for Nora sat upon her table. The books in her library were other people's selections . . . She frequently talked about something being the 'death of her', and certainly anything could have been had she been the first to suffer it.
(p. 99/66)

This rapacity derives from the same human condition suffered by all the characters, the same longing to possess some certainty, some quality that would characterize her: 'She defiled the very meaning of personality in her passion to be a person' (p. 101/67). This condition is only exacerbated by her inability to choose the form she wants to give her life; even her aspirations (the identity she hopes to steal from someone else) are inappropriate, already belonged to some other person. She is equally inappropriate in matters of sex: 'One inevitably thought of her in the act of love emitting florid *commedia dell' arte* ejaculations' (p. 102/68).

Jenny therefore is confused to such a degree that instead of trying in any way to build an identity for herself, she *ex*propriates. Her confusion extends to her suffering, in both senses of the word. She suffers from others' unfulfilled desires, her emotions are 'second-hand' ('she could not participate in a great love, she could only report it'). And she is different from the others in that her suffering is confused in manner: she 'suffers' confusion actively, not passively, her suffering causes pain for other people. 'She was one of the most unimportantly wicked women of her time — because she could not let her time alone, and yet could never be a part of it' (p. 102/67). Thus Jenny's 'sorrow and confusion' are important in the larger context of the book in that they prevent any suspicion of desirability, any hint of distinction, from being attached to the anguish suffered from the awful confusion considered the core of human experience — an anguish shared alike by good and bad.

Of all *Nightwood*'s characters, the doctor is the most conscious that release from this woeful condition can only be found in death: he knows no 'end is sweet' (p. 219/155). His 'safety' from Robin lies in this lucidity: he alone understands her fascination, knows it can offer no relief from the hopelessness of human desire. In a way he has passed beyond desire, in that he expects no satisfaction. As Nora says to him, 'You know what none of us know until we have died. You were dead in the beginning' (p. 214/152).

But lucidity, the consciousness of one's plight, cannot make that plight less bitter — it rather increases the anguish; his wisdom, again in Nora's words, 'is not only the truth, but also the price' (p. 151/90). Knowing that one's desire is hopeless does not stop one from desiring but rather makes the desire more absolute. The doctor's is the most naked pain because it has no object — he alone does not try to limit the scope of his torment by attributing it to any particular source, he alone has not 'dressed the unknowable in the garments of the known' (p. 193/136).

His plight is that of the others, his anguish, like theirs, is related to a 'terrible predicament': 'to be shot for man's meat, but to go down like a girl, crying in the night for her mother' (p. 110/74). This sentence is a blurring of boundaries. The sexes appear a matter of representation only — to others he may appear to be a man but he goes down 'like' a girl. It is interesting to note here that the recurrent inscription of the word 'meat' throughout the novel, with its homonym 'meet' and anagram 'mate', further strengthens this confusion: both men and women desire to be 'man's meat'. But 'meat' is of course to be understood as what man feeds on, as well as what is alive to feed, and love, represented in the book as a carnivorous desire to absorb or devour the other, has no limits in its choice of object: men seek men and women seek women. The sexes are as indistinguishable in their object of desire as they are in their choice of identity.

This confusion of the object acquires a further twist in the 'predicament' quoted above. The slide from passive object (of the shooting; and let us remember that shooting has a specifically masculine sexual connotation) to active subject (going down), effected by the conjunction 'but' (thus both are part of *his* predicament: he is predicated as object and subject, passive and active), confounds any grammatical distinction of the subject.

The doctor shares the same condition of total indeterminacy; like the others, he craves an identity. He wears make-up, women's clothes; he frequently refers to himself in the feminine. Yet he is well aware that he cannot be a woman any more than he can feel himself a man: he must be 'the bearded lady' (p. 145/100). The identity he is seeking is one which would include everything he is not, an identity which would leave him nothing to want: he wants the impossible, and he knows he wants the impossible.

> The wise men say that the remembrance of things past is all that we have for a future, and am I to blame if I've turned up this time as I shouldn't have been, when it was a high soprano I wanted, and deep corn curls to my bum, with a womb as big as the king's kettle, and a bosom as high as the bowsprit of a fishing schooner?
>
> (p. 132/91)

In the doctor's case, therefore, as with the others, the attempt to define an identity is an effort to veil the awfulness of the fundamental 'middle condition', an effort to endow oneself with some definite property — an attempt which he, however, from the outset knows to be doomed to failure. This search for an identity is reflected on other levels in *Nightwood*, notably the racial and the religious; the less conscious the protagonist is of the inescapable futility of desire, the more 'sublime' or sublimated (that is, the less overtly sexual) the quest will be.

O'Connor is the most lucid character and his speeches most indicate that sexual incertitude is the motive force behind every desire. As an example we take his words to Felix.

> 'After all, calamity is what we are all seeking. You have found it. A man is whole only when he takes into account his shadow as well as himself — and what is a man's shadow but his upright astonishment? Guido is the shadow of your anxiety, and Guido's shadow is God's.'

> Felix said: 'Guido also loves women of history.'
> 'Mary's shadow!' said the doctor.
>
> (p. 171–119–20)

On the first reading this seems to have nothing to do with sexual matters; indeed, the passage seems to shed only darkness on what a man's shadow may be, by which plenitude is to be attained. Yet it has sexual overtones which reverberate loudly through the book. It exemplifies the ambiguous use of the word 'man' as subject: 'man' would at first seem to refer only to those of the male sex, since the indefinite article (on the whole?) is not usual when it is understood to include women. However, 'a man's' wholeness is 'what we are all seeking': 'we' is unspecified, a grammatical form; the article inscribes the indefiniteness of what it qualifies — 'man' is, if anything, an indefinite article (not only a woman, Mary, but even anxiety can have a shadow). Man therefore contains woman — yet at the same time is contained in wo–man. Man and woman are inseparable. This reading would seem to be corroborated at another point in the book, for example, when Nora cries that love is 'man seeking his own head? The human head, so rented by misery that even the teeth weigh!' (p. 192/135). Man (and in a reference with specifically sexual connotations) and human — after which the text continues with 'She' — seem interchangeable, as though no precision were possible, as if the only isolable human property were suffering the impossibility of being simply man or woman?

Returning to the quotation, the next question involves the shadow. A man attains plenitude only by taking his shadow into account — what can his shadow be? The part of himself which lies in darkness or the darkness he casts? Is the shadow part of himself or perhaps everything he is not, woman? Is there a boundary between him and his shadow? Is one's shadow of the same sex as oneself, does wholeness imply a conjunction or a disjunction of the sexes? The question is the shadow but the shadow itself is a question, or rather many questions.

The question receives an answer, in the form of a question: 'what is a man's shadow but his upright astonishment?' And this answer too provokes more questions: does this mean a permanent upright position? A posture of miction free from the female 'squatting' position? A permanent erection? Yet 'women of history' are Guido's object of desire and Guido himself (who both is and has a shadow) lacks the (masculine) sexual identity seemingly indicated by such interpretations: the Baron confides to the doctor, 'I have become entangled in the shadow of a vast apprehension which is my son; he is the central point toward which life and death are spinning, the meeting of which my final design will be composed' (p. 168/117).

These questions cannot be resolved. The elaboration offered by the text is itself destabilizing. The passage in its very form creates the confusion it proclaims; its message — that man can only feel 'whole', a unicity (a unicity punctured in turn by the homonymous word 'hole') be established by taking account of one's shadow — is wrought with words

whose meaning immediately wobbles. The most categorical of state-
ments ('A man is whole only when he takes into account his shadow as
well as himself') dissolves into a web of words elusive of any meaning: a
web spun of sexual indeterminacy, where the threads of 'man', 'woman',
'human' entangle any other question.

And the spider in the web is of course Djuna Barnes. *Nightwood* is
written for the same reason that motivates Nora's obsessive need to write
to Robin — 'the extraordinary need of misery to make beauty' (p. 177/
124). As with her characters, Djuna Barnes' misery is one of uncertainty
and confusion, the only escape from which is offered in writing, the
fixing of an illusion: in the Baron's formulation, 'an image is a stop the
mind makes between uncertainties' (p. 160/111). *Nightwood* is written in
the hope that illusion would provide an 'end', as if by creating an image
of the sorrow and confusion of life, she could transcend them. Transcend: they would become the means to an 'end' and her anguish would be
lessened.

Thus it is that early in the book Frau Mann seems able to bear the
awfulness of being human: through her craft she can *mediate* confusion.

> The way she said 'dinner' and the way she said 'champagne' gave
> meat and liquid their exact difference, as if by having surmounted
> two mediums, earth and air, her talent, running forward, achieved
> all others.
>
> (p. 29/14)

She *achieves*, she reaches an end; her craft seems to let her attain an end
by using and passing beyond the 'middle condition' (she has 'sur-
mounted two mediums') where sex is in flux into the realm of illusion.
She can use confusion to create something steady, an image.

Similarly, *Nightwood* is a search for relief from Barnes' anguished
confusion, a search which needs and kneads that confusion but which
can never resolve it. Writing can represent the woe of being alive, the
impossibility of separating man from woman; by giving it form, it can in
one way halt it. But this halt is most of all a perpetuation: writing cannot
give relief, it rather serves to prolong the agony, to extend it into the
realm of illusion, of representation — to render it 'indecently' eternal. As
Nora eventually realizes,

> Looking from her to the Madonna behind the candles, I knew that
> the image, to her, was what I had been to Robin, not a saint at all,
> but a *fixed dismay, the space between the human and the holy head, the
> arena of the 'indecent' eternal.*
>
> (p. 222/157; added emphasis)

Writing, the creation of images, can 'fix', can create something definite
from the 'space between', where being human is itself in question, where

being human is a question of holes. But it can only fix 'dismay'; the 'end' it attains is 'indecent' — would be better off unattained? It was to take nearly twenty years before Djuna Barnes would write again. Perhaps writing *Nightwood* for her was a lesson that 'sorrow and confusion' are rendered only still more woeful by being 'given form'?

8

Jean Genet's *The Miracle of the Rose*

Violette Santellani

Translated from the French by Mairéad Hanrahan

The passage to which this chapter refers is on pages 214/15 of
the Folio edition of *The Miracle of the Rose*, from 'In the colony,
Harcamone was a plasterer and a mason' ('A la colonie,
Harcamone était plâtrier et maçon') to 'He went by in the
Great Square and it was elegance walking arm in arm with
falsehood' ('. . . et c'était, se promenant, l'élégance au bras du
mensonge').

The following is a reading of a passage from Jean Genet's *The Miracle of
the Rose* in which the author, incarcerated in the prison he calls the
'Colony', meets his 'hero', the 18 year-old convict Harcamone, condemned to death for murder.

Genet's description of each of his meetings with Harcamone becomes
a pretext to offer the reader a series of surprising metamorphoses
because of the way he contemplates this being so different from
ourselves, so repugnant to us: the assassin. Genet's account serves to
magnify Harcamone and through his description of the murderer's
suffering we come to recognize ourselves.

The first sentence of the passage seems to set the keynote for a
traditional tale, but Genet almost immediately introduces the interior
scenery of theatrical enchantment which enabled him to avoid being
crushed by his own experience of prison. Harcamone is described as
covered in 'plaster' and this, along with 'powder', represents the props of
the theatrical magic. Suddenly the assassin, whitened, made up, is
transformed into a lunar Pierrot: his face takes on a fixed expression like
the atemporal masks of ancient tragedy.

From this point in the passage we are in the magical forest of love
where an assassin can be transformed into an angel and femininity is
discovered in the most hardened convict.

But careful! Harcamone's white mask hides another face, dark and
sulphurous. As in every apparition of the Wonderful we do not know at
the beginning where the wonder comes from: good or bad? God or Devil?

First, damnation. Our hero limps. He is already victim of an imbalance
and the awkwardness of his body's lop-sided walk is to be found, at
another level, in his fatal mistake: the murder which has shut him up at
18, condemned him to live forever misunderstood in the brief remainder
of an incomprehensible world. Harcamone is nevertheless determined to
live the short time left to him on earth protecting the only thing which is
really his: the image of his body. He knows he is unique as a man, as a
cripple and a criminal, and out of his pride, out of arrogant solitude, he
defends this image of himself.

Genet meets Harcamone, on this page, when he goes outside to
urinate. In the prison universe, it is not without significance that he
should choose this particular moment: an intimate moment of relief in a
world where everything is constraint. It is also a moment in which, in the
homosexual masculine prison-world, man is naked, given over to the
heat and intimacy of his sex and his solitude.

After this, Genet, an ordinary inmate, can 'contemplate' the condemned Harcamone. The same pride brings the two solitudes closer,
that of being — in spite of everything, whatever the weight of the laws, of
history, crushing them — each, a man, and so, unique and desiring:
desirable.

Their meeting takes place as Harcamone crosses the prison courtyard
referred to in the text as 'the Great Square'. This Great Square is the
frame in which Genet places his hero, making an actor of him in a
unique and exemplary drama. It is the theatre, without rehearsal.

Harcamone carries a ladder on his shoulder. Genet's force in writing
this scene is to propose a concrete, visual picture, which he composes
and frames like a painting. The picture will then be transfigured in the
writing, sublimated, as in love or poetic writing.

So, our hero is crossing the Great Square, a ladder on his shoulder. But
which is carrying which? Is the ladder not supporting Harcamone, since
it will serve to deport him, transport him into another frame? Already,
with the inscription of the word 'échelle' ('ladder'), with its feminine
gender, we hear *elle* (she), this first note of femininity which Genet will
use repeatedly as he tells Harcamone's story. The note will transform
Genet into a doe, a saintly Joan of Arc, a wing (*aile*), a female bird (*oiselle*),
to finally blossom in the vision of the Rose.

The story of Harcamone's murder is the story of his passion, of his
Calvary, in the Evangelical sense of the term. A wounded Christ, he
carries the cross which transcends him and saves us. Visually, Harcamone and the ladder together form a cross . . . a cross with wide wings.
These last months, which Harcamone serves in prison knowing he is
condemned to die for his crime, become his justification. They forge his
greatness.

Thus Genet inverts the values of justice and injustice, good and bad.

But . . . 'assassin'; the word is so negatively charged that it makes our hero topple and the Angel, like Lucifer before him, falls out of Paradise. Harcamone is God and the Devil, a fallen God, a lame Devil.

Harcamone's ladder is the balancing bar, the crutch of this new Jacob who cannot see the angels, who has no family, or roots, and who will never find a line, unless here, in the lines of Genet.

In Genet's lines, Harcamone remains brilliant in his wound, encircled with his crime. If he limps (*boîte*), it is also because he is at bay (*aux abois*), an animal wounded by the blood he has spilt . . . the blood of the little girl who has become his blood. Harcamone's action, the action of a new Oedipus, condemns him to die. Through his deed he took what he wanted of the forbidden femininity which the young girl was still too young to give, and which was thus given back to him, as his solitude and his death.

Love or death (*l'amour ou la mort*): for Harcamone everything in the forest is charged with these dangerous, incalculable forces. The difficulty is knowing how to keep one's balance, of keeping, at least, a bridge, a ladder, a hand stretched out to others.

For Harcamone, the bridges are down. For him, the ladder will remain forever suspended between heaven and earth. We can contemplate him like Genet, hold out a flower to him, but to imitate him would be our death.

Genet remains the 14-year-old child . . . at any rate innocent, who had the right to life, who had the right to everything, as it should be for every child, but an orphan . . . but abandoned . . . but imprisoned at the dawn of adolescence . . . who searches and finds love among his prison companions, even the most reprobate. And who remains to write against the law, against the rich, against hypocrites of all sexes and kinds.

The force of his writing is exemplified here in this glimpse of the beauty of a person who, in the last moments of life, blossoms like a rose. Like a rose, on the scaffold Harcamone has the obviousness of existence which does not need justification, which is beautiful, desirable, ephemeral. Ephemeral . . . unless saved by writing, if, as is the case with Genet, others are brought to see and recognize.

9

Spinning form: reading Clarice Lispector

Regina Helena de Oliveira Machado

Translated from the French by Mairéad Hanrahan

This article aims to present a close reading of *A Paixão segundo G.H. (The Passion according to G.H.)*[1] as an exemplary text of the work of Clarice Lispector. It is exemplary in several ways: in that it is itself primarily a putting into form and an exploration of the question of writing; in that it reflects on what giving form is; and in that it is succeeded by texts which will show an even more pronounced 'loss of form'. The writing wants to redeem this loss, yet is worked and crafted by it. It works *on* the loss of form and is worked *by* it.

A querying of form is present throughout *A Paixão segundo G.H.* It could even be said that here this querying is both inaugural and essential: in no other text of Clarice Lispector (although in *A Maça no Escuro*[2] the question can be read implicitly) will one find so explicit and developed a reflection on what 'giving form' may be. It is inaugural in the sense that the movement described by *A Paixão segundo G.H.* can be considered the first, essential movement of all the texts of Clarice Lispector.

This text would thus constitute a sort of originary text, the text of all texts — the earlier and later texts nearly always carry within them the movement of *A Paixão*, this text born of an impulse to understand inseparable from writing or living. It is as though the text of *A Paixão segundo G.H.* were the map, the tracing of the genesis of a person's life — symbolized here by the character G.H. — of that person's relation of comprehension and incomprehension with the world, the other, with language; a relation knotted, instituted, founded in and by the writing which weaves it and of which also it is a basic question. It could be said that *A Paixão segundo G.H.* is questioning form. And the form in question is that taken by a life: the relation between a person (a woman) and her life, that is, whatever calls her to live in a particular way. 'Giving form' is, for the character in the book, 'having a form'.

Form and being thus appear together. Form, before being named writing, is the possibility of existence of what happens to G.H., has happened to her, the life she has led, the life she will lead. Form, in this case writing, is the possibility for someone alive of being in existence. Giving form and forming oneself go together in the same movement.

The character G.H., this woman of whom we shall know little more than the initials of her name, one morning finding herself alone in her apartment (the maid had left the evening before), decides to tidy it, beginning with the maid's room — 'the end of the apartment' — which she expected to revolt her.

One could say that the 'action' begins at the door of the maid's room: on opening the door, G.H. sees the reverse of what she thought she would see. She finds herself before an 'entirely clean' room and instead of the 'indistinct half-light' she had expected, she confronts the 'vision of a room which was a quadrilateral of white light'. Arranged by Janair (the maid) in her own way and with a 'proprietor's audacity', this room was the opposite of everything G.H. had created in her apartment, as if not at all part of it. The maid's room was the very place of light; the place in G.H.'s house which did not belong to her, the foreign place in her home. There, nothing was hers, nothing had been made by her. A place to which she had not given *her* form.

Thus G.H. arrives at the room as if to a world already created without her. From the threshold of this strange place within her own house, the reverse of her apartment, G.H. will begin to face the vision (and the revelation) of the other side of her own life.

At the threshold, from where she sees the room before entering, G.H. is suprised to discover figures drawn on the wall.

> And it was on one of the walls that in a movement of surprise and recoil I saw the unexpected drawing.
>
> On the limewashed walls, adjacent to the door — and that is why I had not yet seen it — was, nearly lifesize the outline in charcoal of a naked man, a naked woman and a dog who was more naked than a dog. In the bodies were not drawn that which nudity reveals,[3] the nudity came simply from the absence of everything which covers: they were the outline of an empty nudity. The strokes were thick, made with a broken tip of charcoal. At places the tracing became double as if one stroke was the tremor of the other. A dry tremor of dry charcoal.
>
> (pp. 38–9)

A sudden, premonitory vision: the figures in black strokes on the white wall are also traces opening up the first pages of the text of her life to

G.H. — an inscription which she is only beginning to decipher, hieroglyphics of an ancient book which she is beginning to read. The writing mimes the stroke of these naked lines, 'as if one stroke was the tremor of the other', and also of the black stroke on the white page, making a double figure as in the drawing.

Like an archaic text, the strokes let themselves be deciphered, their meaning has to be read: 'in the bodies were not drawn that which nudity reveals, the nudity came simply from the absence of everything which covers'. This is the 'empty nudity' which is given to be read, enigmatically. The deciphering: G.H.'s movement of perception, described by the text, is similar to that followed by reading it: as this strange inscription, at first hidden, suddenly emerges into G.H.'s sight, so too the details of the drawing — the three figures emerging little by little as if coming out of the wall — appear in the text, in its lines, in its figures.

Likewise, our reading of the text follows G.H.'s movement of perception before the drawing. What is said of the drawing could be said of the text. G.H. constitutes herself as narrator (and narrated character) of another text on reading the inscription on the wall. Her reading is a writing talking of writing — of the tracing of this inscription on the wall as a writing. And the movement of this reading is itself also a denuding. The room, the drawing, although already naked, allow glimpses — as if through an opening, a groove cut on their surface, a gash or charcoal-stroke — of something, of a hidden 'depth' which they, however, do not have and through which can be perceived fragments of meaning. Although naked, the figures seem still to be uncovering themselves, as if curtains were progressively being raised. But these curtains are perhaps nothing but those of G.H.'s sight, layers and layers of curtains going up from her bare vision, as 'now' she sees.

In this reading, the figures first appear embedded in the wall.

The rigidity of the lines embedded the enlarged, stupid figures in the wall, like those of three automatons. Even the dog had the sweet madness of something not moved by its own force. The poor doing of the overly firm stroke made of the dog something hard and petrified, rather encased in himself than in the wall.

(p. 39)

A relation can be established between what is said of the inscription on the wall and the writing of this text.

The rigidity of the lines is at once the gesture, the mode and the source of the 'act' of inscription. It is what traces, carves, hollows. The rigidity of the inscription, the hardness of the picture — here there is no softness. The gesture is as naked and hard as the petrified dog. The lines are detached from a creative act, the figures are born from lines and strokes

which thus become creative, in the absence of a link with whatever did
the tracing — charcoal or its extension of flesh, the hand. Everything
here permits the reading of a passivity and an autonomy of the figures:
made from the lines which make them. The line is independent, with no
human figure behind the gesture. The only figures are those projected
on the wall by the lines. Nor yet is there humanity in the figures: giant,
stupid, robotlike, at first perceived as endowed with a force which does
not come from themselves, rather they seem machines, haunted dolls
('zombies'), simple mechanisms.

The figures appear to be perceived in this first moment as a 'made
thing': they are detached as figures, from their frame and support (the
wall), in order to loom up, independent. Thus, for example, the dog is
seen as a sculpture rather than as a drawing, 'something hard and
petrified, rather encased in himself than in the wall'. (It is noteworthy
that G.H. sculpted. It was her 'anterior' mode of making form.) The
hardness and the petrifaction, characteristics of stone, reappear in the
dog. The 'poor doing of the stroke' (literally, the 'badly-done', 'o mal-
feito do traco') makes the dog stand out from the stone, defining it, and
makes the stone stand out in the dog who has become not a
representative figure of a live dog but a dog-of-stone. The qualities of
matter — stone, the wall — are thus transposed in the inscription. The
stroke is not merely grafted on to a surface, on to matter which it works,
but is also worked and altered by it. This is accomplished by the 'poor
doing' of the stroke: 'mal-feito', *mal* does, makes, the stroke makes
stone. And the stone, drawing. Again, in the wording of the text there is
an independence of the stroke with regard to an act, a will, the
accomplishment of a doing by a human hand: it is the 'poor doing' of the
stroke which makes the work.

The Inscription

The second moment of G.H.'s perception of the drawing seems to go
even further back in the process of inscription; there is a greater
precision in the noting of what she sees: the rigidity of the figures and
their detachment are associated with the idea of something rising into
view which had been buried. A meaningful link begins to be established
between these atemporal figures and G.H.'s time, movement, present,
life.

> The first surprise once passed of discovering the occult drawing in
> my own house, I examined better, this time with amused surprise,
> the detached figures on the wall. The simplified feet did not get to
> touch the line at the ground, the little heads did not touch the line

of the ceiling — and this, in alliance with the stupefied rigidity of the lines, left the three detached figures like three apparitions of mummies. As more and more the hard immobility of the figures disturbed me, the idea of mummies was getting stronger in me. They were emerging as if they had been a gradual oozing from the interior of the wall, come slowly from the depths to the point of marking the surface of the rough wall with sweat.

(p. 39)

A relation is immediately evident between the art of sculpture, as practised by G.H., and the work of writing. This mural writing is a form working form, as G.H. had discovered in sculpting.

The movement by which the inscription on the wall is given for G.H. to see is interesting in that, like a reading, it pieces together a meaning not given directly. The idea of the apparition, of this appearance from beyond the grave, strengthens the perception of a detachment; dead, the figures acquire the power of phantoms, living again on being evoked (the drawing or writing gives them both death and life). Their detachment figures also the detachment of G.H. who, at this moment in her vision, is detached or turned away from what she sees. But already a link is being woven underground (a link given by the way G.H. relates to the figures, which she animates little by little): in appearing as mummies, in the kind of unburial ascribed to them by G.H., the figures begin to have the power of phantoms; looming up as though from the exterior and from far away, they act in us; dead, they haunt life. The dead figures loom up alive in their independence, as if the inscription, the movement of their unburial, came from themselves, 'come slowly from the depths to the point of marking the surface of the rough wall with sweat'.

The inscription seems to be done from the inside of the wall: the figures appear as if from the other side (from a 'beneath-the-surface') — 'they were emerging as if they had been a gradual oozing from the interior of the wall' — forming the drawing of themselves. A work of matter by matter (of stone by water, for example, as is implicit in the above statement; and the wall moves as does water, it allows emerging, it opens passages like water, it is permeated with water). Water marks the surface (in sweat) as if it was itself tracing the figures.

The idea of a thickness or depth of the surface destroys the classical opposition between surface and depth, or form and depth, opening up to the depth of the surface, or to a form which is itself the depth hollowing into another form.

The figures, nevertheless human, manifest themselves at first detached from every human gesture or figure. The inscription on the wall is made visible in its nudity and detachment, as if rising up out of the infinite. It is the vision of G.H., as expressed by the writing, which in a movement in the opposite direction recomposes the inscription on the wall, even in its appearing.

This primary detachment is also evident in the relation to the frame (the mural frame: the line along the ground, the line of the ceiling), and in the relation of the figures with each other.

> No figure had connections with the other, and the three did not form a group: each figure looked before it, as if it had never looked to the side, as if it had never seen the other and did not know that at the side there was someone.
>
> (p. 39)

The independence and force of dead figures coming to life little by little: their 'automatism' is progressively humanized ('each figure looked', 'and did not know'). The strength of an inscription taking life (looking, knowing) when it is 'read'; the passage of figures coming from the infinite to G.H., the passage of G.H. to each of the figures. The rapport begins to be established at the very moment it is said that there is no rapport: between the figures on the wall, or between G.H. and any other. The drawing is suddenly animated and, reading on, the awakening of G.H. to life now begins, as she emerges from immobility, in a slow unearthing.

> I smiled constrained, I was trying to smile: it is that each figure was there on the wall exactly as I myself had stayed rigid standing at the door of the room. The drawing was not an ornament: it was a writing.
>
> (p. 40)

The revelation of the writing in the drawing on the wall is simultaneous with the vision G.H. has of herself in the figures, the vision of the projected, written image of herself. At the same time as revealing it to her, as denuding her, the drawing reveals itself as a writing. And G.H. can finally read the inscription she had already begun but this identification of herself with the figures on the wall is also a decomposing of the old image; she is beginning to discover herself, seeing herself naked.

Referring to her previous history, to what is being destroyed in her by what is happening, the narrator of *A Paixão* often speaks of 'my civilizations', 'my epoch'. The 'ancestral' writing left on the wall by the maid undermines the 'textual' edifice of G.H., the story, civilization, epoch 'written' in her.

At the same time she is starting to 'see' someone she had never looked at. Like the figures unconnected with each other, she was not aware that someone was there beside her.

The Maid

Something materializes through the inscription — what at first had the ghost-like aspect of an apparition gives way still more to consciousness, in the form of 'memory'. Emerging from the inside of the wall come the reviving memory of the maid and the figure of 'a' G.H. as dead; she, too, a zombie, a phantom, the slave of the image laid bare in the mirror of an inscription left there by the woman she had never noticed beside her: 'the memory of the absent maid was constraining me' (p. 40).

This memory is also gradually put together by the writing; G.H. can now read in herself as if she were pulling the unknown, the repressed, towards consciousness. And the repressed is such that it is as if she had been totally expulsed. The absence of the maid even in her memory is the extent of her own absence. She is as strange to herself (as 'remote') as the maid had been, even when there.

> I wanted to remember her face, and, surprised, I could not — she had so thoroughly excluded me from my own house, as if she had shut the door and left me remote in relation to my own home. The memory of her face escaped me, this had to be a temporary lapse.
>
> (p. 40)

The maid's face emerges slowly, its features at first obscure. But for the first time she is starting to be present for G.H., in this 'forgetful' memory, in this 'lapse' bringing her back. Involved here is the question of absence and presence between the maid and G.H. When present, she had never been so for G.H.: she had remained invisible, dark, as that which absents itself in the unconscious. But now that she is absent, she returns with the strength of presence. But in which writing: her writing? the drawing on the wall? the memory? the text of *A Paixão*? that of G.H., reading, supposed to be writing what she has lived through? that of the one writing G.H.?

> It was not surprising I had used her as if she had no presence: under the little apron, she was always dressed in dark brown or black, which made her completely dark and invisible — I shivered to discover that until now I had never noticed that this woman was an invisible.
>
> (p. 41)

G.H. is now beginning to see what is invisible — in the maid, and in herself.

> And inevitably, such as she was, so must she have seen me? eliminating from my body drawn on the wall everything not essential, and of me too seeing only the contour. However,

curiously, the figure on the wall reminded me of someone, who
was myself.

(p. 41)

The chain of associations bringing the invisible back to the light
finishes by discovering the features of the maid, now traced by the
character G.H. The whole chain is tied up with the inscription: it is the
name which can hollow out the surface of forgetting. While one face
(black, of flesh) remains buried, a face of letters appears.

But her name — of course, of course, I finally remembered: Janair.
And looking at the hieratic drawing, it suddenly occurred to me
that Janair had hated me.

(p. 40)

Janair, the maid, emerges from the drawing where she is invisible as
she who traced the writing to which G.H. is being initiated. She is the
other, the first other whose text is open to G.H., a text where she can
read herself as the other some day would have read her.

For years I had only been judged by my peers and by my own
environment which were, on the whole, made of myself and for
myself. Janair was the first really outside person I was conscious of
looking at me.

(p. 40)

What had first appeared as naked marks, with no author or immediate
sense, becomes writing in G.H.'s reading of it, a hieratic writing, carrying
a message and a judgement. And the judgement is the other's reading of
'me'.

And looking at the hieratic drawing, it suddenly occurred to me
that Janair had hated me. I was looking at the man and woman
figures which held the palms of their vigorous hands exposed and
open and which seemed to have been left there by Janair as a brutal
message for when I would open the door.

(p. 40)

G.H. reads the pages of an accusation; she thus participates in her own
judgement, allowing herself to read, to be read, recognizing herself in
the figures inscribed in Janair's 'text'. In this reading G.H. is rewriting: in
memory retracing Janair's features, she is tracing her own features as she
would have seen them being drawn in the features of the maid. It is
outside herself, in Janair and through her that she first sees herself,
judged and denuded.

My uneasiness was amused, in a certain way: never before had it
occurred to me that in Janair's muteness there could be censure of

my life, which must have been called 'a men's life' by her silence?
how had she judged me?

(p. 40)

The first signs of an unknown 'self' or 'ego' echo, making sense and
flesh of the she who is still almost nobody. In the silence (muteness) of
the other, 'I' hears: 'a men's life'. The construction of the statement is a
formulation of the passage from one to the other (from the maid's vision
to that of G.H.). Thus one notices, within the same statement, that the
affirmative phrase (the supposition) is transformed into the interrogative,
as if the enunciation was shifting between 'seeing' from Janair's
viewpoint and seeing that point of view with a certain distance (she does
not entirely affirm Janair's point of view but puts it into question at the
end of the statement).

'Man' is the first signifier of this laying bare, the first projected image
of a 'self' hitherto neuter, almost without genre, just as it has no body, no
history.

> I act like what is called a realised person. Having done some
> sculpture during an indeterminate and intermittent time gave me
> also a past and a present which meant that others situate me. I am
> referred to as to someone who does sculptures that would not be
> bad if there was less amateurism. For a woman, this reputation is a
> lot socially and it situated me, for others as much as for myself, in a
> zone which, socially, is between woman and man.

(p. 25)

Realization in life and art, in a life which is an art and in an 'almost'
accomplished art (her work is 'not bad') — this realization, socially
speaking, makes a sexually indefinite person out of G.H. She uses her sex
like a dress, a present she had neither asked nor paid for, like a thing
given her without struggle or conquest. Being a woman was a gift and
had the gratuitousness and facility of gifts; something which did not
involve her, did not entail a commitment on her part.

> And as for men and women, what was I? I have always had an
> extremely affectionate admiration for masculine customs and ways,
> and without urgency I had the pleasure of being feminine, being
> feminine for me has also been a gift. I only had the facility of gifts
> and not the amazement of vocations — is that it?

(p. 28)

It is only in the maid's room, before the mural inscription, that for the
first time G.H. is going to be called to answer for herself. Excluded from
her own house, far from her home (this 'simply artistic creation'), her
image uncovered, she will now have to look for the path, first traced by

Janair, which will lead her to herself. The figures projected on the wall first send her back the image of Man.

> I looked at the wall where I had to be being portrayed . . . Me, the Man. And as for the dog — would that be the epithet she was giving me?
>
> (p. 40)

Man, the dog, these are the first words of a sentence G.H. hears from the judgement she attributes to Janair. Thus she is first judged at the crossing in the human species of humanity and animality.

Only later she will recognize herself as *she*. But this will be the *she* she will become by passing through the 'judgement of herself'. She will come to let herself be formed by the room and the occult life of the room only by losing her previous form.

> Naked, as if prepared for the entrance of one single person. And whoever enters would be transformed into a 'she' or a 'he'. I was the one the room was calling 'she'.
>
> (p. 60)

In letting herself be judged, crossed through by these others, 'he's and 'she's, the unknown occupants of the room and of herself — the man, the dog, the maid — she will finally recognize herself in the marks of the naked woman ('I was drawing back in myself to the wall where I was incrusting myself on the drawing of the woman' (p. 64)). The passage from G.H. to woman can only be reached after the appearance of the other occupant of the room: the only other presence alive in the book, less 'humanised', less domestic than a dog, an animal which would never be represented beside a man and a woman: the cockroach. But before arriving at that point, G.H. has to experience her loss and her passion. What the narrator terms a depersonalization, a deheroization, can only be attained through such a painful, laborious approach to the other.

★   ★   ★

The hero, in the texts of Clarice Lispector, is the individual who distinguishes himself absolutely from others, from the community, the common run of men, either by a gesture, an action (a crime, as in the case of Martim in *A Maça no Escuro*) or by some encounter which results in an event (as is the case with G.H. coming across a 'nothing', a cockroach, in her apartment). Such an action or encounter destroys the previous lives of these characters who then find themselves apart from other men. They have 'seen' and experienced something which does not belong in 'humanised', 'sentimentalised' everyday life. There is a movement of heroization which begins with an 'exit', a rupture. The characters who thus lose their form and their anterior life begin by creating themselves as gods. The hero trades with the absolute. In this 'creation', he constitutes himself, exteriorizes himself, tends towards an objectivity. These are the heroes of depersonalization — a fact which may seem paradoxical: dispossession of the self brings a dividend for the self (Martim becomes a hero, G.H. understands that she wanted to realize the 'maximum' act). Deheroization here is the ultimate accomplishment of the dispossession of the self, the final blow to the last wiles of the ego, which, as Freud said, is the real hero of every narration.[4]

Another path of research opens with the question of deheroization in the text of Clarice Lispector, the question of 'genre'. The 'hero' here seems to be a typically masculine figure. While his work is one of construction, of reparation of an originary loss (in the character's history and in the writing), deheroization is going to be the labour of destruction of the construction, an 'underground' labour (being done from the inside out and from underneath the construction) which enables us to see the gap in the lives of the characters and in the text itself through what the narrator of A Paixão calls the 'rupture' (fracasso) of language. In the movement of deheroization, therefore, there would be something of the nature of an unburial of the originary loss — that which is the reason both for the writing and for the construction. Perhaps here is where one can speak of a femininity in Clarice Lispector's texts: the writing is born of fissure and of loss and, to pursue the metaphor further, one could say that it is born of what is most maternal in construction and in language, a breach in the body of a construction, whether the wall of the maid's room or the construction of language and of the text. It is born of that point where language is opening, where it gives place, is a passage to something new. Yet 'creating' oneself, wanting to construct is not enough to become a hero. Heroism has an essential relation with speech, it is tied to the fact of wanting to speak, of understanding, or wanting to make oneself understood. G.H.'s relation with the world is given by the writing of this book, from the outset she is a prey to silence. The test of speech and of its failure follows her from the beginning of the text. She fails the test of her 'heroism' yet she gains deheroization and renunciation, in recompense, as a victory.

G.H. does want to speak. And perhaps it is through speech and its failure that she rejoins Martim. G.H. breaks the silence with a cry which could pull 'thousands of beings' along with it.

Everything was ferociously summed up in never uttering a first cry — a first cry unleashes all the others, the first cry in being born unleashes a life, if I cried I would awaken thousands of crying beings who would initiate on the roofs a choir of cries and horror.
(p. 63)

Likewise, Martim discovers that his greatest crime had been his 'heroism'. 'In a world of silence, he had spoken.' Martim's deheroization consists of speaking less and less. Like the narrator of *A Paixão*, for whom deheroization is the 'failure of the voice'.

Silence, or 'muteness', is the common point between these two movements of deheroization. The same is true for other Clarician characters who also see and experience something not belonging to 'everyday life'. They too do not speak, but what they do not voice as characters is said by the cries of the text before it too returns to silence.

★   ★   ★

In *A Paixão segundo G.H.* and many other of Clarice Lispector's texts, something occurs and becomes an event which disorganizes life, reality, meaning and the subject who experiences it. In *A Paixão* a cockroach is concerned, but elsewhere a rat, or a blind man, a beggar, a bandit . . . The occurrence thus provokes a disorganization, a loss of form which is at the origin of the writing: the writing subject tries to understand (to put in form by and in writing) what is happening to it. Thus the subject is disorganized from the start. Writing, giving form, in this sense, is an effort to understand what is happening, with an attempt at reorganization.

But this 'putting in form', this 'understanding' must at the same time respect the occurrence as such, in its sudden unexpectedness, in its strangeness and its otherness, without appropriating it, integrating it, neutralizing it. This is the particularly ethical requirement of Clarice Lispector's writing with regard to what is taking place. Thus is moves forward by moving back; comes nearer by withdrawing; gives form by letting the formless, the incomprehensible inscribe itself. To receive the other in its otherness, the writing gives form while at the same time respecting formlessness, the other which is incomprehensible for the self, the other which is absolutely other. Therefore it cannot give *its* form to the other. The other 'for me', is the absence of form. This is why the writing is elaborated as an art of failure, an art of withdrawal, as giving form in a freer, delicate, unconscious movement, inattentively. Inattentive enough, far enough away, for the formless, the incomprehensible, to be able to leave its own traces. And this is the point of celebration, where there is sharing in the mystery of whatever happens, of the incidental, in the mystery of the incomprehensible.

A thread stretches from one of Clarice Lispector's texts to another, at times with interruptions. There was already a 'thread of water' in *Perto do Coração Selvagem*.[5] There is the thread of water of *Agua Viva*,[6] here and there transformed into a thread of steel, or to the 'delicate threads of a spider's web', or a thread of yarn. Sewing thread, weaving thread. Sometimes a line of fire, a line of metal or of flesh, a horizon line, or the line holding the bait which will try to seek in speaking what is not speech, not the word: between the lines. Or again the thread of a 'toothache', woven through *A Hora da Estrela*.[7]

There is always the trace of, and work on, thread, in the texts of Clarice Lispector, in these texts which are woven with thread, or which, as one would say for a life, hang by a thread.

But a thread seems to be interrupted with *A Paixão segundo G.H.*. Or to put it differently, after this text, the space between lines, or non-speaking, seems definitively incorporated into the words of Clarice. After this text, so implacably and uninterruptedly linked together, there seems to be a movement turning more and more towards a shattering of form. Her work opens up, gives place much more to the fragment, to a more and more free, spaced text, a text let loose, bearing the marks of incomprehension and of silence, of the unknown including that of speech, of a not-knowing-how-to-say ('There are many things to say which I do not know how to say. The words are lacking', 'I do not know what I am writing about: I am obscure for myself', 'What shall I say to you? I shall say the instants to you', *Agua Viva*). More and more writing makes way for the lack of words, for silence in words, for the lack of construction ('I want the experience of a lack of construction').

If *A Paixão* was the impossible narrative of a loss of form, the failure of construction, a loss which the writing still sought to understand, to 'form', the later texts (notably *Agua Viva, A Hora da Estrela, Um Sopro de Vida*)[8] are the progressively more pronounced inscription of this loss of unity (of the subject, of form even as a printed book) and of the opening up to the unknown and incomprehensible which the last pages of *A Paixão* were already embracing ('I do not understand what I am saying, never! never again will I understand what I say . . . And so I adore').

The last texts are constructed on the thread of time, *Agua Viva* on the flow of instants, of the division and fragmentation of the instant.

> My theme is the instant? my theme of life. I want to be like it, I divide myself thousands of times in as many times as [there are] instants flowing, fragmentary that I am and precarious the moments — I lay myself open only to life which is born with time and grows with it: it is only in time that there is space for me.'
>
> (*Agua Viva*)

A Hora da Estrela is constructed as a 'gradual vision' of what the narrator does not yet know: 'It is the vision of the imminence of. Of what? Who knows if later I shall know.' Writing, then, is at the edge, the 'edge of'; announcing itself in this way and carrying in it the mark of this proximity, the mark of something which is not said, but which weaves through the text like a hidden thread. Ever nearer silence ('Everything I write is forged in my silence and half-darkness'), the writing works its own 'desisting', it dangerously goes on working, digging the 'gap', the 'fissure', accentuating the movement of renunciation, of withdrawal.

The possibility of stopping is evident more often within the text itself: 'I write or do not write?' And occasionally the sentences stop, unfinished: 'I would have liked.' (*Um Sopro de Vida*).

There is a relation between the extreme experience of 'letting go' in *A Paixão* and the increasingly marked inscription of fragmentation, unfinishedness, incomprehension, loss of form, of language, of self in the later texts. There is a continuity of losing (written at length in *A Paixão*) which is prolonged and aggravated in the other texts which are, wrought by it — or un-wrought. And this is so not merely with regard to narrative form, which undoes itself (*Agua Viva* is already the book of a thousand instants and stories, like so many texts within the text) but with regard to the very fabric of the text. The text itself is going to be written on 'remains'; not only in actually speaking of what can be called 'remains' and what the narrator of *A Paixão* herself calls 'remains' — a cockroach in an empty room or an event erupting into orderly daily life — but also written *on* remnants of paper of every sort (so the text will be an inscription *on* the remnant, the remnant itself a support), that is, on scraps of notebooks, envelopes, napkins, wastepaper, fragments of 'yellowed white matter' heaped up anyhow until, the writing exhausted, there remains to be done only the piecing together of the text with its losses, the 'unleashed' text. The work of 'concatenation', as Clarice Lispector would say. The assembling and weaving of the remains, the remnants. This is the case with *Agua Viva* and will be the case, in a more extreme manner, with *A Hora da Estrela* and *Um Sopro de Vida*, the last texts.

The writing progressively stops speaking, crying out its silence, the muteness towards which it dizzily flings itself.

Notes

1. *A Paixão segundo G.H.*, Rio de Janeiro, Editora do Autor, 1964. All page references are to this edition and all quotations have been translated by the translator in consultation with the contributor.
2. *A Maça no Escuro*, São Paulo, Editora Circulo do Livro, 1961. Translated into English as *The Apple in the Dark*, Gregory Rabassa, London, Virago, 1985.
3. Literally, the first phrase of the statement is in the plural ('In the bodies *were* not drawn'), disagreeing with the second ('that which nudity reveals') but agreeing implicitly with the plural of what nudity reveals, that is, the sexes.
4. The feeling of security with which I follow the hero through his perilous adventures is the same as the feeling with which a hero in real life throws

himself into the water to save a drowning man or exposes himself to the
enemy's fire in order to storm a battery. It is the true heroic feeling, which one
of our best writers [Anzengruber] has expressed in an inimitable phrase:
'Nothing can happen to *me*!' It seems to me, however, that through this
revealing characteristic of invulnerability we can immediately recognize His
Majesty the Ego, the hero alike of every day-dream and of every story. (S.
Freud, 'Creative writers and day-dreaming' (1908), in the *Standard Edition of the
Complete Psychological Works of Sigmund Freud*, translated by J. Strachey,
vol. IX, pp. 149–50, London, Hogarth Press and the Institute of Psychoanaly-
sis.)

5. *Perto do Coração Selvagem* (Near to the Wild Heart), Rio de Janeiro, Editora
Fronteira, 1944.
6. *Agua Viva*, São Paulo, Circulo do Livro S.A., 1976.
7. Translated into English as *The Hour of the Star*, Giovanni Pontiero,
Manchester, Carcanet, 1986.
8. *Um Sopro de Vida*, (A Breath of Life), Rio de Janeiro, Editora Nova Fronteira,
1978.

10

Hélène Cixous' *Ou l'art de l'innocence*: the path to you

Pierre Salesne

Translated from the French by Mairéad Hanrahan

In Hélène Cixous' *Ou l'art de l'innocence*[1] and *Limonade tout était si infini*[2] a new point of questioning is reached. After *Illa*[3] which elaborated a myth of writing originating in the body, *Ou l'art de l'innocence* progresses further and goes directly to the birthplace of the writing.

These texts propose a meditation on creation, a reflection on the conditions of writing. *Ou l'art de l'innocence* examines how writing works by asking all the questions posed for anyone torn by the impulse to live and the impulse to write, when the questions are those agitating a woman concerned with being a woman today, historically as well as poetically. What relation exists between living and writing? What produces the act of writing? What are the obligations binding on anyone who wants her writing to remain in close contact with life? What conditions allow life to emerge in a text? Life and writing cannot be separated; aesthetics and ethics are closely bound.

Ou l'art de l'innocence brings together in its title some of the questions posed by the text. What is an art of innocence? Can innocence be an art, can an art be innocent? Can one speak of innocence in writing? What would be the nature of such an innocence and of an art which would make possible the bringing together of these apparently antagonistic terms?

The title itself is put in question. In this case can one still speak of a title in the classical sense of the term, as if somehow it encapsulated the work? This title subverts its very function: it is disturbing because it is presented as part of a process already begun. It does not stop; on the contrary it indicates a circulatory, evolutionary process. The uncompleted title bewitches grammar, it *de*grammarizes, restoring to language a suppleness and ludic quality: *Ou l'art de l'innocence* is full of humour.

The coordinating particle *Ou* (*Or*) at the start invites the reader to speculate on what precedes the title; *Ou* transforms the title into a mobile which sets the whole of the text in motion: it allows the inaudible (the silence indicated by the coordinating particle) to be heard. *Or* becomes synonymous with the very breath of life: 'It is the non–noise of the voice between two tones' (p. 254).

Ou also expresses the ambivalence of the narrator before writing.

> Do I sacrifice love to writing yes or no, do I sacrifice the near to the far away yesorno, do I sacrifice air to the word, yesno or noyes, do I sacrifice the thing to the name, no or yes, and the non–name to the name, and one minute to the other, yes, no and laws to beyonds: yes or no.
>
> (p. 244)

All the narrator's questions have their origin in the insistent *or* of this quotation: 'My questions are all of *Or*' (p. 253). *Or* is the ambivalent conjunction which both joins and disjoins. *Or* is hated when it separates too forcefully but loved when it effects transition.

> But sometimes I love the word *or* like the air I breathe, when I pass from one thought to another thought.
>
> (p. 254)

Thus in the title of the book, *Or* has a value of circulation and exchange, at the limit of silence. The writing of the title *de*-nominates — here with a double meaning: the prefix 'de'- also indicates distance, separation, deprivation (as in de-plete).

Furthermore, the title on the cover does not correspond to that of the title page, *With ou l'art de l'innocence* (*With or the Art of Innocence*). This displacement from one title to another shows that the effect of the title is illusory. Between the two titles a supplement 'With' is added which disturbs and 'estranges', that is, makes strange, as much by the language as by its location. This supplement 'With' invites further speculation on the signification of the title.

The presence of a word in another language brings into question the very value of strangeness or foreignness: this positive value given to strangeness is a constant in the texts of Hélène Cixous. 'With' also emphasizes the blessing of feeling a language strange within one, as she says in *La Venue à l'écriture*:[4]

> In my language foreign languages are my sources, my emotions. 'Foreign': music in me from elsewhere: a precious warning: don't forget that everything is not here . . . see the innumerable, listen to the untranslatable.
>
> (p. 28)

The presence of foreign languages prevents the author from establishing 'ownership' over her language, from appropriating it. Recourse to the signifier 'With' opens her language up and enables it to overflow in dialogue with other languages. Thus for a French ear, the beginning of 'With' pronounced aloud evokes the word 'oui' (yes) which could be one of the titles of *Ou l'art de l'innocence*: 'oui' as synonymous with saying 'with'.

But the signifier 'With', combined with the signifier 'ou' (or), enriches the title at the intersection of the two languages. 'With' coupled with the following word 'ou' lets the English word 'without' ring out. The English inscribes the 'with' which it eliminates. It would nearly be necessary to say 'with without'.

These plays on language, on signifiers, on places, are in no way gratuitous. They are in fact efforts to realize an art of innocence: the combining of the extreme refinement of art (its long technical elaboration) with the lightness of innocence. The equivalence established between 'with' and the art of innocence is shaken by the use of two languages in the title: this equivalence also enables 'without' to have a voice. Hélène Cixous wants to let the present moment live in her writing: 'With' is what already exists before writing, the living moment, the present.

> This not–yet–written book already existed? Already existed, coming
> from your hands, from another language, speaking to me already.
> > (p. 172)

'With' would be the stretched out hand of life, looking for the hand of writing, looking to be written by it.

With came and said 'are you writing me?' (p. 173).

The path of writing would lead from one silence to another: from the nameless 'with' to its naming, a naming of silence as a sigh, as the preservation of what is most alive.

> Forgive me for having given you a name to call you towards me.
> Forget it, I beg you . . .
> I say to you: come. Come without a name between us. There will
> be no place for a name when you are near you.
> > (p. 309)

Ou l'art de l'innocence is therefore the very difficult attempt to write in innocence. Writing is the ambivalent place which allows life at its extreme limit to be described, perceived, reflected on, and yet which at the same time is always suspected of being incapable of a close rendering of the aliveness of reality.

Why can I not write far from myself, far from paper! Dictate to my
friend what writing dictates to me, without losing the sea.

(p. 275)

The paradox of the title and its mystery underline the difficulty of such
an act of writing.

This book is very difficult. Because it is a book which wants at the
same time its living and its writing.

(p. 173)

Ou l'art de l'innocence textualizes the conflict between writing and
living. This struggle is written and lived particularly violently in the
subject H.C.[5], both author and character of the text; because this relation
to 'writing–living' is where, for Hélène Cixous, the truth of works of art
is defined:

I think that the truth of literature turns on the struggle between the
value of life and the value of writing.[6]

Writing and living intersect; for some it is a combat, for others a
process of substitution or a love-relation. The discreet but constant
presence of Kafka in the texts of Hélène Cixous is a result of the
singularly sharp feeling he had of the conflict between writing and life.
For Kafka, writing meant abandoning the world, sacrifice. Writing
stopped Kafka from getting married, from having children or from
leading his life in conformity with the ideal of tradition and his
education. For him, writing was a fault. His numerous broken engage-
ments and the deep sense of guilt he felt about them, as well as the
substantial evidence he left in his writings (the *Diary*, the *Letters to Felice*),
tell of the extent to which this conflict tore him apart. He had to sacrifice
his daily life and his body in order to write.

Hélène Cixous refuses to sacrifice life to writing or writing to life. This
determination animates the desire of the 'book of presents':

I want to write the epic of the presents and I want to live with dash
and with dotted precision . . . And also: I want to write the book of
an instant, I want to write book–instants.

(p. 239)

In *Ou l'art de l'innocence*, writing is considered as a vocation, religious
(answering a divine call) as well as poetical, taken as a metaphor
(answering a voice in oneself). This vocation does not only apply to
writing but concerns every form of investment which contends with
love. Whether writing has come to H.C. or H.C. has entered writing as
one enters an order or a party, writing is in every case experienced as a
'giving oneself up to'. But this gift, this present which is also a luxury,

must also be put in question. The danger for a writer is to take him or herself for Orpheus and to drive Eurydice back into hell.

> And here is where she asks herself again cruelly and severely if she is not still more often Orpheus than Eurydice, which is her most hostile suspicion. H. — I must suspect myself to the point of falling sick from it. I have to drug myself on suspicion. Otherwise I forgive myself so quickly the suspicion would rather be a caress than a question-blow. (This story of being Orpheus-Eurydice is my wolf, it is to frighten me enough.)
>
> (p. 121)

The contradiction of writing, her *felix culpa* (the Augustinian expression borrowed by Joyce to describe the work of art or its origin, sin being transformed into a happy production) animates the writing of Hélène Cixous.

> I think: what is spoken is lost; and on the other hand I think: what is not spoken is lost differently.
>
> (p. 244)

> I cannot live without writing; and I cannot live without making love. But the difference is the distance between bodies. Between writing and caressing you, cold catches me.
>
> (p. 279)

The risk for H.C. is to take herself for a writer. Thus writing should be borrowed like a ladder of paper to attain the greater-than-self:

> I do not write to arrive, but to remove myself. I write to transport my lives far from my edges, to what is mystery for me, and there, trembling, I still write.
>
> (p. 279)

It must not be forgotten that 'writing is not an end'. 'Writing is an only writing' (p. 261).

The happiness obtained by writing, by the discovery of 'regions of jubilation', is both paradisiac and infernal because it touches the limit between you and without you. For Hélène Cixous, writing is born of the need for encounter with a universal you. Her aim is this naming of the other, the inscription of the life of you in the text. But there is a great risk that in this quest of you, the subject H.C., having to draw away from herself, her ego, should also lose the meeting with the other.

> This hour of happiness is deadly for me. I write to go further than myself; but what anguish if I reach there! Far from me, I can only bear it if you will take me in your arms.
>
> (p. 27)

Besides this negative or restrictive message, the writing carries a
positive one because it struggles against the mortal muteness which
threatens everyone who feels forbidden to speak. Writing is also a
liberation, the surging up of all forbidden words. 'I write to un–silence,
not to speak' (p. 279). Un–silence: to make the ancient, unknown voice
of the self ring out, the archaic voice, the one singing in each of us. 'I
always hear a sombre, warm voice in the depths of the past' (p. 278).
Writing is above all the trace left by the expulsion of this voice in oneself,
a nameless voice.

> I don't know where it is going, but I learn it every time I hear the
> Voice my beloved, a sombre, heavy Voice with big, calm breasts
> calls my life, come, calls my life to call it, it is always the Voice–self,
> my life must have heard it before my memory saw daylight, but my
> night remembers.
>
> (p. 118)

The voice of language also makes us hear 'unearth' in 'unsilence'.[7]
And writing is also this work of unburial, this struggle against forgetting,
this refusal to give in to a passivity which would play the game of death.

> For me living is always being sur/prised[8] at death's jealousy . . . The
> trap is its indolence, which wins us, by definition, without effort.
> Because dying is always given to us, it is living that has to be taken:
> morning and evening I say to myself, take three breaths of life and
> undie lively.
>
> (p. 256)

Writing, by its slower approach, allows one to seize the ever fleeting
instants of reality.

> I write . . . to slow down, to approach, plunged in writing where
> everything can be listened to infinitely more slowly. But I am not
> unknowing: there are approaches which increase distance. Delay-
> ing can give life, give death.
>
> (p. 261)

A movement of tension and exchange is produced between writing
and living.

> I need to write, I need to surprise myself living: I need to feel myself
> shuddering with life: I need to call myself to live and to answer
> myself living: I need to live in the present of the present: I need to
> doublelive; I need to take life; I'm scared writing might take itself
> for living; I need writing to think of living: I write to celebrate

living: I need to accompany living with a music: I need writing to
fête living.

(p. 256)

The close association of living and writing to be read in the
composition of this paragraph is accentuated even more by the
anaphoral 'I need'.

Need is the name of my vital discovery.

(p. 289)

One only needs need to begin to discover.

(p. 290)

The ultimate wish of writing would be the text of pure life: the
moment where writing would efface itself before life. The ultimate
question of *Ou l'art de l'innocence* is that of the vital, necessary relation
between words and silence, where words operate as the guardian of
silence.

Everything that is written loses silence and everything is written by
losing breath. But the silence is not lost, it keeps itself just beside.

(p. 261)

The supreme paradox and sublime ambition of the writing would be
to reach, to win, to have the right to silence, but to a silence which would
not be a silence of before-speaking but a silence of after-speaking.

I want to arrive, to the end, to the place where the silence which all
languages make, throwing themselves in the sea, echoes.

(p. 99)

In the formal organization of *Ou l'art de l'innocence* we can also find
attempts to transcribe these moments touching silence. Thus at one
moment where the subject H.C. takes an initiatory plunge into Paradise
and discovers the mystery of living, the text is passed to a feminine
character: Amyriam,who retranscribes for H.C. what can only be
murmured:

'. . .' (A note from Amyriam: everything following is more guessed
than understood. H., her body bent in two, no longer speaks: is
pouring tears of words. Calls living 'a being born within'. Her
interior voice at times colourless, at times shining and black.
Throws black flashes. A large part of what follows ' ' is a
reconstitution.)

(p. 203)

In the same way, the end of the book is not written as an end, that is, an interruption, a finish, but as an opening towards silence as beginning.

> I listen to ending beginning by a silence another song'.
>
> (p. 307)

> H. — I have finished. But some words are still being written above the paper, in the following silence.
>
> (p. 308)

In what follows this passage, the feminine characters, including the narrator, dissolve. There is a moment of writing delivered without being attributed to a source.

> — — There is no longer anyone here. Nobody stayed to sign. They all went to live outside the programme. Some extremely transgressive lives.
>
> (P. 310)

The author splits in two, becomes, like the letter of her first name H., a breath.

> — —I look at *us* and perched beside this moment I see myself look at us live-so-much, so existing, so threatened, so superbly free, so intense, so escaped, so actual.
>
> (p. 310; added emphasis)

The previously quoted 'note from Amyriam' and this last quotation can serve as examples of the work on writing carried out by H.C. These moments exceed the classical boundary of writing. This requires working not only on language but also on punctuation, on the very syntax of the sentence. In the 'note from Amyriam' let us underline again the absence of a grammatical subject in the second sentence: 'calls living "a being born within"'. A purely nominal sentence follows. Through its graphic arrangement the writing seeks to transcribe the movements, in the almost physical sense, of body and soul. In order to write a text without a subject, a pure text, whose narration in the present can be secured neither by the subject of the action nor by a witness or omniscient narrator, the text has recourse to the use of silent graphic notations: quotation marks surrounding silence, '   ', or the double dash of the last quotation which subverts the usual function of the single dash (the mark of a return to a unique speaker). The second dash may be said to be the initial of silence.

Let us further evoke the unusual use of pronouns: where 'I' is at once included in and excluded from 'we', where 'I' loses its unique status to become plural and allows perception of what a culture delivered from the restraints of languages might be.

Uncounted, untranslatable languages, offering a common grammatical feature: the existence of a personal singular plural instinc-
tive pronoun endowed with vaso-dilator often cosmic properties.
(p. 91)

But H.C. cannot receive this writing free of limits simply: it provokes a
question.

My real problem is perhaps that . . . I cannot live without posing
myself the question;
'Could I live without writing?' and without leaving it unanswered.
(p. 238)

What art would be sufficiently diaphanous and subtle to give
expression to reality? What writing is most faithful to life? How to say
the true — what Hélène Cixous enjoys calling 'quasacles (quasi-miracles
of instants)'? How to write what is both the simplest, because it is reality
itself, and the most difficult, because reality exceeds what can be said of it
and can find itself covered over by its representation?
One of the difficulties for H.C. is that this book of presents and
happinesses can only be written in total dispossession.

I would like to write like a fish in writing, entirely adopted by the
sea . . . I dream of being able to have living writing surprised by the
other, of not-taking it.

(p. 275)

But the innocence of this art must not be confused with naivety or
ignorance: rather it is situated beyond knowledge, in a knowledge of
non-knowledge, obtained at the price of a long labour of the soul, of
reflection on language and on the very body of the sentence.

Innocence is when, after a work of indescribable mathematicity, by
dint of living life at extremely close quarters, and of weighing-
querying every scruple of living, and of weighing every result of
thinking and rethinking and sublimating and replunging in the
struggle, and the earth, and shuffling and sifting, and dis and
entangling every step of life, a sincerity hatches to a single white
dreamy petal. It is the simplicity at the end of all chemistries.
(p. 141)

The innocence of writing therefore involves labour: the questioning of
the complexities and conventions in which writing loses an innocence it
may (questionably) have had. Hélène Cixous' texts are born of the very
movement of the urge to write: a movement which disorders and
explodes novelistic order. *Ou l'art de l'innocence* is written not in any one
genre or gender but where they overflow.

> How strange it is to meet the thought which teaches me, today that
> I have never written (never known? never wanted? been able? been
> obliged . . . ?) *a* story with *a* beginning, its continuation, its halts,
> changing with correspondence etc. . . and arrival.
>
> Nor *a* book either, is that not so? I have never been able to write 'a
> book', with an end which ends, a finished end, with a last step at the
> end.[9]
>
> (p. 51)

The refusal to write in an assigned gender, to tell a story inscribed in a
particular code, is in relation to the questions of 'difference' in libidinal
economy at work in the writing. *Ou l'art de l'innocence* is presented as the
text of 'femininity' in writing. This difference in libidinal economy can
be read in the differences of behaviour with regard to the preservation of
the self, the spending of the self, and the relation to the other.

Writing is produced in overflowing the logic of discourse, leaving
place for restlessness and for questioning. Inscribing an end and a
beginning would mean that the author must come back to the origin of
her book after its completion; an initial moment of exit would be
succeeded by a movement of re-entering the text, aimed at reappropriat-
ing and controlling the path travelled. Hélène Cixous refuses the
movement of detachment between writing and the writing subject which
makes of the latter the reader of his or her own text, correcting it
afterwards and mastering it.

> I have never been able to turn around. I have never been able to
> write with reading following the text and dragging it along.
>
> (p. 52)

She explains this impossibility by a difference in the imaginary whose
source is the body.

> I am a woman. I am a being for whom being born is a going out and
> not a going in.
>
> (p. 53)

Here the question of gender crosses that of engendering. Her metaphor
for writing is above all that of birth. The act of writing concerns
something passing through the subject, something figured by a movement of egress.

To stay close to the living, the writing subject is divided into several
personae (Antouilya, Amyriam, Aura, Cordelia, Nuriel). These do not
appear to have the structure of characters in a novel with a psychology of
their own: they are rather potentialities of the ego, the writing 'I'. This
division allows Hélène Cixous to express the different beings peopling
or crossing through each of us. The book is written like an opera, in a

sequence of dialogues where each voice questions, answers, takes up a theme again or moves away from it, summons other voices. Sometimes the identity of the voice is specified, at other times the dialogue is marked only by a single dash indicating a change of speaker or merely a change in the register of idea of the same speaker.

This polyphony decentres *Ou l'art de l'innocence* and produces a circulatory movement organized in accordance not with a narrative order but with a melodic movement. The code of representation is also subverted. These personae are not represented: they acquire form with the actual writing of the text. They are not enclosed *a priori* in any story. Thus while Cordelia's presence is particularly prominent in the first quarter of the book, she disappears later on, without anything announcing her disappearance. She is present while the narrator is dealing with her own resistances: when this is no longer the case, *Ou l'art de l'innocence* follows a path of life and thought where Cordelia has no place. Aura on the contrary comes and goes; her existence reaches beyond the book. She was there already before the written work and continues after the end. Twice, however, when H. goes into regions of being or writing which are not linked to Aura, she disappears, first for forty pages, then for sixty pages.

Studying Cordelia and Aura allows us to appreciate that *Ou l'art de l'innocence* is not written linearly towards an aim defined in advance. The text is produced following a double rhythm, one metonymical in which a word, a thought, leads to another, the other making us hear the hammering of repetition. The text develops organically: the movements of thought in it are closely related to their inscription in the body: 'She has an extremely corporeal soul' (p. 49). Each moment of the text finds its natural completion. This can be the end of a breath, an experience or a thought.

> Now the coming-chapter arrives by itself at its ending. Because it is time.
> What H. has been learning for some months is that things finish each in their own way, arrive at their end, end by arriving there, each at its hour, the flower at its hour-of-flower, and the chapter at its hour of thought, and enjoyment at its hour of love and onto lips, peacefully. And it's good.
>
> (p. 222)

Sometimes the cuts between moments are marked explicitly:

> And the dream came with its explanation.
> (End of the first part of this thought.)
>
> (p. 95)

At other times a gap alone indicates the change.

Even if the cuts are natural, they are queried. They can be a point of contradiction or hesitation for the narrator. There is a great temptation for her to continue a thought after its completion by setting it moving again with new questions. And the greatest difficulty can be sensing the moment a thought reaches its hour of completion.

> It is very difficult in the case of thoughts which plunge so far away to know if they turn us away from or bring us nearer to our object. It is necessary to know how to break a charm delicately. So I think: Here would begin the second part of the detouring thought about Aura's sources.
>
> (p. 95)

The general figure of *Ou l'art de l'innocence* is that of a quest: writing is experienced as an initiatory route across the topography of the living where H.C. goes forward in the light of questions. The book is of questions, the book itself is in question.

> There are not answers which answer but there are answers which question.
>
> (p. 79)

Seeking neither to say nor to represent, Hélène Cixous abandons herself to writing. As she says in *La Jeune Née*,[10]

> Writing is in me the crossing, entry, exit, sojourn, of the other that I am and am not, that I don't know how to be, but that I feel pass through, that makes me live, — that tears me, worries me, alters me, who? — one, one, some?[11], several, the unknown which gives me precisely the wish to know from which all life surges forth.
>
> (p. 158)

This abandon gives place to the other, it gives birth: abandon is closely conjugated with femininity. In *Ou l'art de l'innocence*, Hélène Cixous is carried away, transported, as she follows the writing being written.

> Everything I write wrote itself, I have always been carried away on board a nervous writingship veering with the wind, coming I don't know from where.
>
> (p. 53)

The writing is experienced as an annunciation, a promise of a birth to be awaited. Waiting, 'woman's art', is welcoming the unknown, life, love, what will be and 'what dictates to me inside': mystery.

> Waiting begins thus: standing, pregnant, with whom? straight and quiet the palms of the feet stuck like ears to the earth's breast, with

musical hips, at the window of day, light is pregnant, with whom, you will see, waiting smiles, listens to silence pregnant with things, with a delicate listening, listens to things growing preparing themselves to appear and begins continuously with A.

(p. 35)

Waiting is the first step on the path to the unknown, to mystery. And this mystery is first linked with the body, then with woman:

Mystery is always of the body.
Mystery is always of the body of a woman.

(p. 199)

Mystery is discovered as a continuous engendering: the text moves towards a new genesis of life and of creation in a rhapsody elaborated around three words: mystery, body, woman. The secret of mystery is, like woman, at the origin already to be 'full of others'. The richness of mystery or of 'woman' is being inhabited by the unknown, being full of the mystery of You, in an unignorant ignorance.

A woman is with-woman. Is with. Is with.[12] There is a woman in a woman . . .

(p. 203)

In writing's approach, H.C. discovers the passion of You. Writing for Hélène Cixous is a Jacob's ladder which leads her towards the You around which circle all her texts:

All the books I could write turn around the book which I shall never write and which causes all the others to be written, and this book of books is the book of You.

(p 201)

In *Ou l'art de l'innocence* this You (greater than 'I' yet felt by H.C. within her) is still idealized, still irrepresentable. To write the book of You, the hand of writing needs the hand of You to take body. In Hélène Cixous' later work, this hand does come: it is called Promethea and the book is *The Book of Promethea*. Other hands follow, those of the theatre, those of the Cambodian people, those of Winnie and Nelson Mandela. And Hélène Cixous continues.

Notes

1. *Ou l'art de l'innocence* (*Or the Art of Innocence*), Paris, Editions des femmes, 1981. (No English translation is available.) All page references are to this edition and all quotations from this and all other works cited have been translated by the translator in consultation with Hélène Cixous.

2. *Limonade tout était si infini*, Paris, Editions des femmes, 1982. (*Lemonade Everything was so Infinite,* translated by A. Liddle, is pending publication with Editions des femmes.)

3. *Illa*, Paris, Editions des femmes, 1980.

4. *La Venue à l'écriture*, Paris, Union Générale d'Editions, Collection 10/18, 1977.

5. By H.C. we designate, to distinguish her from Hélène Cixous, the narrator of *Ou l'art de l'innocence*. We note that there are at least four positions of enunciation which concern the author; Hélène Cixous, the author; H.C., the narrator; H., which is the initial used by the other characters to designate the character who is writing. It is also the initial used in the dialogued forms of the book, therefore a final instance which has no name and refers to a neuter narrative form.

6. Interview with Hélène Cixous, H. Quéré, 'Le Roman aujourd'hui', *Fabula*, no. 3, Paris, 1984.

7. Unearth (*déterre*) and unsilence (*détaire*) are homophonous in French.

8. Textually: 'over/taken', from the French *sur/prendre*. Hélène Cixous emphasizes the intensive value of the prefix *sur-* (e.g. charge/surcharge).

9. The insistent exchange between masculine (*un*) and feminine (*une*) is unfortunately lost in English.

10. *La Jeune Née*, Paris, Union Générale d'Editions, Collection 10/18, 1975.

11. '(U)ne, un, des?': the play of the original inscribes the diversity of gender of the indefinite article, and the plurality of the singular.

12. The second 'with' is in English in the original.

11

Hélène Cixous' *Le Livre de Promethea:* Paradise refound

Sarah Cornell

J'ai des difficultés avec ce livre. Mais ce livre n'en a pas avec lui-même, ni avec Promethea.

Pourquoi j'ai peur? Parce que c'est un livre pour Enfants. Enfants avec Grand E. Enfants Grands. De toutes les générations et races et genres.

Parce que c'est un livre d'amour. Je l'appelle parfois le Livre des Furieurs. C'est un livre furieux. On doit s'y jeter. Une fois dans le feu, on est baigné de douceur.

Parce que c'est un livre de maintenant . . . à lire sans calcul. Sans demander: 'et après? et à la fin?' Car il n'y en a pas.

Parce que c'est un livre qui n'a pas peur. D'ailleurs c'est ce qui fait que H n'aurait pas pu l'écrire seule. Et moi non plus.

I have difficulties with this book. But this book does not have any with itself, nor with Promethea.

Why am I afraid? Because this is a book for Children. Children with a Big C. Big Children. Of all generations and races and genders.

Because this is a book of love. I sometimes call it the Book of Furies. This is a furious book. You must throw yourself in. Once in the fire, you are bathed in gentleness.

Because this is a book of now . . . to be read without calculation. Without asking: 'and afterwards? and at the end?' For there is none.

Because this is a book that is not afraid. Besides, this is the reason H could not have written it alone. And neither could I.

D'ailleurs c'est le livre de Promethea. C'est le livre que Promethea a allumé comme un incendie dans l'âme de H.

Promethea ne comprend pas pourquoi j'ai laissé entrer H ici alors que le livre était déjà si florissant et verdoyant autour de nous. Je ne sais pas comment me justifier. Je n'ai pas pu faire autrement. Il y a des moments où je suis H. Je n'y tiens pas. Je cherche seulement à ne pas couper le cours du texte, même si je suis presque évanouie dans une fureur.

Mais le plus souvent l'évanouie, c'est H.

J'ai dit que c'est un livre entièrement intérieur. Si l'auteur que je suis éprouve le besoin de fabriquer un boulevard extérieur ou une échelle ou de tisser une tente de soie ce n'est peut-être pas à son honneur.

Promethea est mon héroïne.
Mais la question de l'écriture est mon adversaire.
Promethea est l'héroïne de ma vie, de mon imagination, de mon livre.
Je suis sa championne. Je me bats pour elle, pour faire triompher son droit: sa réalité, sa présence, sa grandeur. Je suis armée d'amour, d'attention. Ça ne suffit pas.

Parfois j'ai aussi besoin d'ajouter l'écriture. Promethea est si grande. L'écriture m'aide. Je grimpe sur elle.

Mais l'écriture me demande aussitôt un salaire, et je ne sais pas exactement en quoi il consiste.

Il se passe des choses étranges: j'écris pour m'approcher de Promethea, je la cherche mieux, plus lentement, de plus près, plus profondément. Mais alors je commence à perdre la surface, la simplicité, la lumière.

C'est le drame.
Cela peut aller loin. Cela peut aller trop loin.
Il se passe d'autres choses étranges: chaque page que j'écris pourrait être la première page du livre. Chaque page est tout à fait en droit d'être la première page. Comment est-ce possible?

Cela tient à ce que ce livre est un jour après jour, et chaque jour est le jour principal, celui qui est en train de se passer. J'ai besoin de tout le temps pour chaque jour.

Parce que nous sommes dans l'éternité.
Nous. Promethea, moi, l'auteur, H, vous, toi, qui veut, qui nous aime, qui aime.

Ce livre est un ensemble de premières pages.
C'est un drame, pour l'auteur.
Et aussi parfois c'est un souci douloureux. J'ai mal à la tête pour cela: je voudrais que Promethea choisisse une page qui serait la première, comme on choisit un coquillage sur la plage.

Besides, this is the book of Promethea. This is the book that Promethea lit like a blaze in the soul of H.

Promethea does not understand why I let H enter here whereas the book is already so flourishing and verdant round about us. I do not know how to justify myself. I could not do otherwise. There are moments when I am H. I would rather not be. I am only seeking not to cut the course of the text, even if I have almost fainted away in a fury.

But more often than not, the one who faints away is H.

I said that this is an entirely interior book. If the author I am feels the need to fabricate an exterior boulevard or a ladder or weave a silk tent, this is perhaps not to her honour.

Promethea is my heroine.

But the question of writing is my adversary.

Promethea is the heroine of my life, of my imagination, of my book.

I am her champion. I fight for her, to make her right triumph: her reality, her presence, her grandeur.

I am armed with love, with attention. This does not suffice.

Sometimes I also need to add writing. Promethea is so grand. Writing helps me. I climb up on it.

But writing asks me for a salary immediately and I do not know exactly what it consists of.

Strange things happen: I write to draw closer to Promethea, I seek her out better, more slowly, more closely, more profoundly. But then I begin to lose the surface, the simplicity, the light.

It is dramatic.

That can go far. That can go too far.

Other strange things happen: each page that I write could be the first page of the book. Each page is completely entitled to be the first page. How is this possible?

That is due to the fact that this book is a day after day, and each day is the principal day, the one that is happening. I need all our time for each day.

Because we are in eternity.

We. Promethea, me, the author, H, you, thou, whoever wants to, whoever loves us, whoever loves.

This book is an ensemble of first pages.

This is a dramatic situation for the author.

And also sometimes this is a painful worry. I have a headache because of that: I would like Promethea to choose a page that would be the first one, like a shell is chosen on the beach.[1]

Ever since the publication of her first fictional text, *Le Prénom de Dieu*[2] in 1967, Hélène Cixous has produced a prolific oeuvre made up of fiction, theatre, and theoretical, literary and poetic essays. Within the wide range of this creative diversity, the works of fiction have constituted the major portion of the overall textual corpus up until recent years. Published in 1983, *Le Livre de Promethea* is situated in an important pivotal period, where Cixous' general orientation is shifting from the writing of fiction towards writing for the theatre.

As the inscription of a significant turning point, how does *Le Livre de Promethea* illustrate the effects of metamorphosis in the general course of the work? What fundamental questions arise concerning the practice of writing? What is the author's status? What are the relationships and borderlines between living and writing? Between reality and fiction? This essay will attempt to address itself to these questions.

A Founding Metaphor: Paradise Lost

The question of Paradise Lost has been a principal *leitmotif* throughout Hélène Cixous' work. It remains ever present in her most recent play, *L'Histoire terrible mais inachevée de Norodom Sihanouk, roi du Cambodge*,[3] where the tragic destiny of the Cambodian people incarnates a modern day metaphor of Paradise Lost. This engendering theme is rooted in Hélène Cixous' personal history; as she explains in 'From the scene of the unconscious to the scene of history', Paradise Lost is linked to her experience of growing up as a Jewish child in Algeria.

> In the beginning, there was for me and there is for me *Paradise Lost*. This paradise had a name, Algeria, that I lived in the present and about which I felt through infantile prophecy, through the anticipation of all my senses, that it was already the country of memory.[4]

The ineluctable expulsion from paradise is at the very origin of the desire to write.

> You want — To Write? Ownership, entitlement had always policed me: I learned to speak French in a garden from which I was on the point of being expelled because I was Jewish. I was of the race of the losers of paradise.[5]

Following the loss of paradise, writing becomes a transgressive way of repairing the separation, of carrying out the work of mourning. It is a vehicle, a means of transport, of crossing through hell in search of a second paradise.

I believe that one can only begin to advance on the path of discovery, of discovery of writing or of anything else from mourning and in the reparation of mourning. Originally, the gesture of writing is linked to the experience of disappearance, to the feeling of having lost the key to the world, of having been thrown outside. Of now having to acquire the precious sense of the rare, of the mortal. Of having to find again, urgently, the entry, the breath, to keep the trace.[6]

The fictional texts written prior to *Le Livre de Promethea* exemplify this quest 'to keep the trace', to find the entry into paradise again.[7]

Hell is incomprehension, it's the redoubtable mystery, the devilish and demoniac feeling of being nothing, of controlling nothing, of being in the unformed, of being tiny in front of the immense. And also of being bad and sometimes even mean. Our meanness is one of the vertiginous themes that opens the space of writing.

One writes to leave this hell in direction towards the hidden day. One writes towards what is going to turn out at last to be the present. Paradise is that, it's managing to live the present.[8]

The Promethean Work of Love: Recreating Paradise with the Other

Le Livre de Promethea explores the question of 'managing to live the present' through the newly found 'paradise' of a love relationship. It recounts the incessant daily process of finding, losing, refinding, and regaining the paradise of the present, of 'now'.

It is also 'a book of love'. Paradise is living the present, but it is also living the immediate non-deferred happiness of paradise with the other. *Le Livre de Promethea* is about the discovery of the Promised Land, about the unhoped for encounter with the humanly divine other: Promethea.[9]

Living in paradise requires a superhuman Promethean effort in order to surpass one's own limits.

Living alive in paradise demands a superhuman endeavour ... when I speak about paradise, today, I'm thinking about the one that must be made with the strengths we don't have and that must be invented; I think about the garden that must be created above the known earth with earth that must be found. I think about the plants and about the forests that must not only be grown but that we must know how to name, nourish, love. Because in order to make a paradise live, we must unceasingly think about it, want it again,

every day water it with tears and walk about it, praising it and
encouraging it. There is no paradise that holds up without the
contribution of tender daily care.

(p. 75)

This effort, coupled with the constant fear of losing paradise again,
can, in fact, turn paradise into hell. 'I'm here now. And it's hell. Paradise?
Yes, I'm still here. But who?' (p. 50).

'. . . but who is the author? Hélène Cixous? H? or Promethea?'

This quotation is taken from the back cover of *Le Livre de Promethea*.
Inasmuch as the reader's initial approach to a text usually begins at this
outermost edge of a book, the author will often choose to present
particularly significant content matter at this location. But in this case,
there is a question: 'who is the author?' Who will choose? Who will
choose who is who? The very question of the 'author's' identity is the
first question asked by the text. It is a question which remains open-
ended, becoming a source of momentum and unbounded narrative
mobility throughout the entire book. 'I have difficulties with this book.
But this book doesn't have any with itself, nor with Promethea.'

The 'I' narrating here is presumably the 'author's' voice. However, 'I' is
rather more complex than might be expected.

When I say 'I', it's never the subject of an autobiography, my I is
free. Is the subject of my madness, of my states of alarm, of my
vertigo.

I is the heroine of my furies, of my uncertainties, of my passions.
I abandons herself. I abandon myself. I surrenders, loses herself,
doesn't understand herself. Has nothing to say about me . . .

I can speak about Promethea without any limit — other than that
of the reader's lassitude.

But about me? No. Who could speak about 'me', if it's not me
and if I am the 'author'?

This is a burning question. I don't have an answer yet personally.

(pp. 27–28)

The delicate vacillation between the first and third persons frees the 'I'
from the constraints of the autobiographical literary gender: 'When I say
"I", it's never the subject of an autobiography, my I is free.' 'I' is a self-
effaced narrating voice, capable of fainting away completely as subject,
leaving behind only the trace of its verbal movement during moments of
excess: 'Is the subject of my madness, of my states of alarm, of my
vertigo.'

At other times, 'I' is externalized from the 'author' as the 'heroine' acting out states of high emotional intensity: 'I is the heroine of my furies, of my uncertainties, of my passions.' 'I' lets herself be transported as far as possible from the conservative narcissistic ego. In releasing herself from the rational mastery of the ego, and in adventuring out to the extreme limits of her proper borders, the 'I' is depersonalized, and slides into a position of exchanging transformation with a more detached third person subject: 'I abandons herself. I abandon myself. I surrenders, loses herself, doesn't understand herself.'

The 'I' doesn't speak for the egotistical 'me': 'Has nothing to say about me.' This process of dispossession, of 'de-egoization' ('démoisation'), of distancing from the self-centred ego, creates room for the other. As a result, the author can become the place of the other's inscription. This position of active passivity will become increasingly important for Hélène Cixous when creating characters for the theatre.

> (O)ne must reach this state of 'démoisation'; this state of without-the-ego, of dispossession of the ego, which is going to make the *possession* of the author by the characters possible. The author had this bewildering experience. In writing the play, *L'Histoire terrible mais inachevée de Norodom Sihanouk, roi du Cambodge*, all of a sudden, I was invaded by a whole people and by very precise people I didn't know at all and who became my relatives for eternity. I discovered afterwards that this was exactly what happened to the actor. The true actor is someone who has an ego reserved enough, humble enough, so that the other can invade him and occupy him; he is the place for the other in an unbelievable manner.[10]

Le Livre de Promethea, however, is not a play. It is a 'book' where the author is present as writer and protagonist. Therefore, the process of dispossession creates a paradox for the author.

> I can speak about Promethea without any limit — other than that of the reader's lassitude.
> But about me? No. Who could speak about 'me', if it's not me and if I am the 'author'?

If 'I' is in a perpetual state of transformation, depersonalization and displacement from the ego,

> who could speak about 'me', if it's not me and if I am the 'author'?
> This is a burning question. I don't have any answer yet personally.

The author leaves the question open and, in a deliberately humorous way, remains 'personally' undecided about the answer.

The complexity of the narrative voice is extended by another phenomenom which Promethea does not understand and the author does not know how to justify: the 'author' is split in two, divided into 'I' and 'H':

> Promethea doesn't understand why I let H enter here whereas the book is already so flourishing and verdant round about us. I don't know how to justify myself. I couldn't do otherwise There are moments when I am H. I'd rather not be. I'm only seeking not to cut the course of the text, even if I have almost fainted away in a fury.
>
> But more often than not, the one who faints away is H.

This presents another problem of identity for the reader: who is H? The author has two places in the text.

> I had reserved myself two places in the text (in order to be able to slide unceasingly from one to the other)
>
> (p. 19)

Being able to 'slide unceasingly' from one position to another offers the writer maximal narrative mobility. It guarantees continuity even when the narrating 'I' is passionately carried away to the point of disappearance. 'I'm only seeking not to cut the course of the text, even if I have almost fainted away in a fury.' Inversely, it permits H to faint away in the same manner: 'But more often that not, the one who faints away is H.'

This possibility of 'trading places' creates a metamorphic connecting flow between the moments of disappearance and reappearance of I and/ or H. It enhances the transformational nature of the many blank spaces provided by the fragmentary style of the textual surface, in which H may faint away into a blank space and then resurface in the text as I, or vice versa.

Moreover, the splitting of the subject allows I to search for a solution to her 'maddening question':

> My maddening question is: What is to be done in order to be simultaneously in the interior and at the exterior?
>
> (p. 23)

The first pages of *Le Livre de Promethea* furnish an example of attempting simultaneous double positioning on the inside and on the outside of the text. H is already 'inside' the book whereas I has just arrived 'outside' the book to try to do the introduction;

> This is not a preface. It's a little tiny chance to say the truth about the origin of this text from which I have just arrived refreshed, jostled, and also submerged.
>
> (p. 11)

Adopting a different dual position, the author can also 'take *both* sides' and playfully debate over the pros and cons of establishing this introductory exterior edge. On the one hand, she actively undertakes the work of 'trying to do an introduction (p. 11) which would serve as 'the most suitable entry' (p. 14) to this book which 'is already' (p. 14); while, on the other, she expresses her doubts about feeling the need to do so since the book is 'entirely interior'.

> I said that this is an entirely interior book. If the author I am feels the need to fabricate an exterior boulevard or a ladder or weave a silk tent, this is perhaps not to her honour.

Living and Writing

The positive division between H and I allows the author to develop the question of the relationship between living and writing. The possibility of being two suspends the necessity of choosing to be the writing *or* the living subject. The author's inclination is to try to be both at once.

> I must try to ask the question of my division between I and H.
> I'm asking Promethea the permission to be a bit two, or a bit more, a bit uncertain as long as I have not succeeded in accepting to live and to write exactly there where I live, and thus to simply be myself the same one who lives and writes — or to really make up my mind in favour of one of my two possibilities.
> I'm inclined towards union, at this moment . . .
>
> (pp. 18–19)

The exchanging proximity between living and writing has never before been so ardently questioned as in *Le Livre de Promethea*. The author's newly aroused incertitude stems from Promethea's unexpected arrival, which has brought a whole new life to live.

> Suddenly it's no longer the same life at all: it's as if I had been flowing in my bed towards death, amply, patiently, forty-five years, and now she descends upon me from the top of her mountain, she falls with all her strength as if the mountain itself had been transformed into water, and she throws herself into my life on a Monday of February, with all her brilliant waves which swell my soul up over my banks and spill me over
>
> (p. 52)

The flooding movement produced by the sudden presence of the other, and of a new life, disorients the author and sets her out in search of shores (or edges) from which she can write: 'And me now, where am I living? On what shores am I going to write?' (p. 182).

The author desires to maintain non-oppositional 'overflowing' between life and writing in order to ensure that one will not repress the other. However, in trying to attain this new interlacing adhesion between life and writing, everything is transformed: the author's life, the author herself, and her writing.

> This book is too difficult to do for the one I used to be. Everything has become difficult for me. I now live beyond my strength, I must conquer each minute of my life which has become immense and free and savage, and all new. This life, I don't know how to live it. I was never taught. No one had spoken to me about these turbulences. I believe I believed 'loving' to be the gentlest and easiest thing in the world. It is not at all that. I had not been told about the storms, about the squalls on the edge of the abyss, about the eclipses of the sun
>
> (p. 53)

For the author she is now, 'everything has become difficult', both living and writing. First, she must learn to live her all-new turbulent life of loving, while trying to deal with the many difficulties that arise from the writing of Le Livre de Promethea.

'The question of writing is my adversary.'

The difficulties confronting the author are largely created by a sudden necessity to radically change her way of writing. A previous practice of writing can no longer be contained within the former fictional limits. A close reading of an opening section of Le Livre de Promethea (the passage translated at the beginning of this essay) illustrates these general difficulties.

The first difficulty comes back to the question of 'who is the author?'. While 'the author' per se tries to come to terms with her role and status, she tells us that Promethea is the originating source of the book: 'this is the book of Promethea.' The 'author' makes no appropriating or authorative claim to the book. The book exceeds both her will-power and mastery. It is the book 'of' as well as the book 'from' Promethea. (The French de of Le Livre de Promethea plays on this oscillation between provenance and belonging.)

This is the book that Promethea lit like a blaze in the soul of H.

The allusion to the Promethean gift of fire underlines the contribution of the other in the conception and the spreading of the book. The hearth of H's soul (and not her mind) houses the blaze lit by Promethea and the book springs forth from within. Before this the author wrote her books alone.

> I have new problems with this book: because up until the present time, I am the one who did my books in majority . . .
>
> (p. 20)

The enormous difference with *Le Livre de Promethea* is that neither 'I' nor 'H' could have written it alone: 'H couldn't have written it alone. And neither could I.'

The book is a present received from Promethea and the 'author' does not wish to keep the gift for herself. She gives the present again and keeps the gift circulating: 'I have already said that this book is from Promethea. It comes to me from her and I want it to return to her' (p. 51).

Other difficulties for the writer consist in her mixed feelings about her new partial role in 'doing' this book. Her 'sense of responsibility' and ethical principles are a source of worry and fear.

> I feel ill at ease, almost unemployed, a little touchy, very gay, insouciance tempts me, the idea of hardly being the author of the book that precedes me, ravishes me and frightens me. I do have the sense of responsibility. I especially do not want to be the abusive beneficiary of a work of which I am only a part.
>
> (p. 20)

Moreover, the shared authorship of the book has altered the relationship between fiction and reality for the writer.

> I am — I was up until now — an author who always tried to transform reality into fiction, through equal respect for reality and for fiction, I felt obliged to keep myself away from any attempt at representation and for that I always wanted to keep writing at some distance from life itself (at least this is what I believed I wanted to do — but I can't judge the result).
> I tried to write properly . . . Etc.
>
> (p. 19)

Instead of trying 'to *transform* reality into fiction', the writer must now attempt to faithfully cross them together. She can no longer 'keep writing at some distance from life itself' because she has been invaded by a new life and the reality of Promethea which is now so close.

> I open my notebook, I open the window, I call out, and my heroine is here, in reality. I'm overwhelmed by it.

I warn her: 'I'm writing on you, Promethea, flee, save yourself. I'm afraid of writing you, I'm going to wound you!'.

But instead of fleeing, she arrives at a gallop, she enters out of breath through the window, and all alive throws herself into the book, and there are bursts of laughter and splashes of water everywhere, on my notebook, on the table, on my hands, on our bodies.

(p. 23)

The amusing nature of the above passage does not cancel out the writer's fear of writing (on) Promethea. Since a certain kind of writing could potentially wound her heroine, the writer personifies the question of writing as her 'adversary'.

Promethea is my heroine.
But the question of writing is my adversary.
Promethea is the heroine of my life, of my imagination, of my book.
I am her champion. I fight for her, to make her right triumph: her reality, her presence, her grandeur.
I am armed with love, with attention. This doesn't suffice.
Sometimes I also need to add writing. Promethea is so grand. Writing helps me. I climb up on it.

But writing is dangerous. It can disfigure or deform 'her reality, her presence, her grandeur'. Writing must not cover Promethea with words. 'It is repugnant to me to make her up with words ('la *maquiller* de mots')' (p. 22).

The writer uses writing as a helpful means of transportation to approach Promethea.

I write to draw closer to Promethea, I seek her out better, more slowly, more closely, more profoundly. But then I begin to lose the surface, the simplicity, the light.
It's dramatic.
That can go far. That can go too far.

Without the immediate presence of Promethea, writing can, on the contrary, carry the writer away from Promethea, away from the simple surface adjoining fiction and reality, or, even worse, away from truth: 'I'm afraid, if she's not here, that writing will carry me away from her, far from me, far from writing, far from the truth' (p. 23). The writer must struggle to bridle writing and keep it in step with the reality of Promethea's presence.

Still another difficulty, (this time qualified as 'a dramatic situation for the author') is rooted in the fact that *Le Livre de Promethea* 'is a book entirely in the present' (p. 23).

> (E)ach page that I write could be the first page of the book. Each page is completely entitled to be the first page. How is this possible?
>
> That is due to the fact that this book is a day after day, and each day is the principal day, the one that is happening. I need all our time for each day.
>
> Because we are in eternity.
>
> We. Promethea, me, the author, H, you, thou, whoever wants to, whoever loves us, whoever loves.
>
> This book is an ensemble of first pages.
>
> This is a dramatic situation for the author.
>
> And also sometimes this is a painful worry. I have a headache because of that . . .

This book, composed of 'an ensemble of first pages', differs from the more linear pattern of development employed in previous texts to work through a problematic question. The writer must resolve the new problem of ordering present moments of eternity. The book defies all laws of hierarchical or chronological order: 'this book is a day after day, and each day is the principal day, the one that is happening.'

Who, then, will choose the arrangement of the textual sequence? 'I would like Promethea to choose a page that would be the first one, like a shell on the beach.'

Le Livre de Promethea: The Book of Books

Le Livre de Promethea itself acts out the perpetual transformation of life. The text constantly shifts from one state to another, from one realm to another, one subject to another. The book is ever changing.

> (T)his is a book calling for children . . . this is a book of love . . . I sometimes call it the Book of Furies. This is a furious book . . . This is a book of now . . . this is a book that is not afraid . . . This is the book of Promethea. This is the book Promethea lit like a blaze in the soul of H.

Through its metonymic movement, this permutative series demonstrates the gliding transformational process at work in *Le Livre de Promethea*. The free flowing style is characteristic of the freedom of the book itself: the book is free ('le livre est libre'). There is an originary re-joining between *livre* and *libre*, two words which share the same etymological roots in the Latin *liber*. Not only is the book *free*, it is also *freed* (délivré). It is delivered, un-booked, unbound: 'an ensemble of first pages'.

Notes

1. Hélène Cixous, *Le Livre de Promethea*, Paris, Editions Gallimard, 1983, pp. 20–22. (No English translation available.) The passage quoted was translated by the contributor. All the following references to this translation will appear without endnote numbers.
2. Hélène Cixous, *Le Prénom de Dieu*, Paris, Editions Bernard Grasset, 1967.
3. Hélène Cixous, *L'Histoire terrible mais inachevée de Norodom Sihanouk, roi du Cambodge*, Paris, Editions du Théâtre du Soleil, 1985. The first performance of the play was presented by the Théâtre du Soleil at the Cartoucherie on 11 September 1985.
4. Hélène Cixous, 'De la scène de l'inconscient à la scène de l'histoire', p. 1. (Lecture given in French at the Institut Français in Copenhagen on 6 May 1986.) Passages quoted here were translated by the contributor. An unabridged English translation is shortly to be published by *New Literary History* (University of Virginia Press). The original French version is pending publication.
5. Hélène Cixous, *La Venue à l'écriture*, Paris, Union Générale d'Editions, Collection 10/18, 1977, p. 20.
6. 'De la scène de l'inconscient à la scène de l'histoire', p. 6.
7. In order to initiate this schematic movement towards the paradise of living the present, Hélène Cixous' text may open with a leading question denoting uncertainty or anxiety, introducing the general direction of the development to follow. The first lines of *Souffles*, for example, ask the question of living in the present in relation to the birth of 'whom': 'And now, who to be born? (Et maintenant, qui naître?)' (*Souffles*, Paris, Editions des femmes, 1975, p. 9.) *Anankè* also begins with the question of living the present, this time in relation to place: 'And now your life, where now (. . .)?' (*Anankè*, Paris, Editions des femmes, 1979, p. 9.)
8. 'De la scène de l'inconscient à la scène de l'histoire', p. 9.
9. The polysemia of Promethea's name evokes both the *prom*ise and the *Prom*ised land, as well as the Greek 'divine goddess', *thea*.
10. 'De la scène de l'inconscient à la scène de l'histoire', pp. 17–18.

12

Conversations

(The following text is the result of two tape-recorded conversations with Hélène Cixous and the other contributors to this volume about the work of the research seminar. The conversations, which were recorded in French, took place at Hélène Cixous' home in Paris over two Saturdays during April 1986. They have been compiled and translated by Susan Sellers.)

Hélène Cixous: I'll begin with the word joy.

I begin with joy though the word I noted down while you were talking was 'war'?

Why did I note the word 'war'?

I have lived with the text since my earliest childhood. From the time I knew how to read it has saved me. The fact that there are books saved me from the war and violence which existed in the countries I come from. Then, when I was an adult, I realized that this world of writing and literature was threatened. I realized it was in the process of disappearing under the bombardment of all those who use language as their weapon, turning it against people, against the heart, in a destructive and dishonest way. Something had to be saved.

I see our seminar as a place where each person who comes to it, comes as a guardian of the text, of the rich potential of languages, of the miraculous phenomenon writing is. I use the word 'guardian' — Kafka's word — not just in the passive sense, but as someone who breathes on the fire, runs to fetch fuel for it: fosterer of the vital flame.

We work together. In one of the oldest texts in the world — the Sumerian epic of Gilgamesh — Gilgamesh and Enkidu set out together to discover the secret of life and death. Throughout the text there is a rhyme like a refrain: 'alone I can do nothing but together we can do anything'. It might seem a platitude, but it's the first literary inscription in the world. It's 'give me your hand so that I may go and discover the secret of life and death'. I desire that hand.

Working together, our seminar is constituted as a group of people almost 'religiously', in the etymological sense of the word. Our 'religion' is a religion of thinking. What groups us together is our desire to think and our belief that thinking is best done in a group, that one thought helps another to advance. I believe thinking is most powerful when it is poetic. Strictly speaking, thought has philosophy as its synonym. But philosophy proceeds in a manner which I find restrictive. I prefer thinking in a poetic overflowing.

Our mission is collective. We work to keep alive the memory not just of what has been, but of what is. The texts help us to remember. We find in the texts of Rilke or Clarice Lispector, for example, the means to rekindle the memory of the most everyday thing — the thing that is most beautiful, the most subject to obliteration: it might be the mystery of a rose. In the seminar we work on the innumerable mysteries that create life, the mysteries that we always forget as they lose themselves, caught in the uproar of our daily lives.

I have an image of the seminar as a country floating above all the countries in the world. It's a country made up of volunteers, of people who want to be a part of it. It's thus a country beyond frontiers and nationalisms and police laws, beyond capitalization and literary order, a country on the side of freedom, where we talk from one language to another, from one civilization to another, from one memory to the other.

Pierre Salesne: For me, the seminar is a place of encounter and it's the desire for encounter, and exchange, which I find so stimulating.

I see my work both as a constant battle and as a source of infinite pleasure. I see it as a battle against all the prohibitions I recognize within myself as well as those imposed on me by society. Alone I am incapable of fighting against these barriers. Working together collectively on a text it's as if there are hands held out towards me, giving me the strength to fight.

Nadia Setti: I noted the word *vivaio* in Italian (which means 'seed-bed' or 'breeding-ground'), a place where embryos of all kinds germinate and grow. Here, we 'cultivate' poems, texts. Our work consists not only in raising questions but also in ploughing, sowing. We are inspired in this work not only by our love of poetry, but also by our belief that what we do nourishes something vital.

Violette Santellani: The poetry we are concerned with in the seminar could be described as the opposite of the lie. It's the act of 'stepping out' — a stepping out propelled by a childlike innocence, the sort of innocence which is capable of knowing and writing those moments of our genuine bedazzlement, the truths which are the most difficult to think and bring to life, the magnificent, vital, terrifying questions of life and death, so fundamental to our human condition and yet so consistently repressed.

Sarah Cornell: I believe that it is fair to say that one of the basic passwords of our work is *giving*: *giving up* narcissistic arms of self-defence; *giving in* to the urge to let go and to try to approach the text differently; finally *giving again* what we have received from the text to others. Giving again or transmitting the gift received from the text is, of course, a meaningful experience of pleasure, but it also constitutes the fundamental ethical reason for our work together.

Mara Négron Marreo: I see our work as a form of protection, the saving of something living and true. It's a grain of sand compared to the world we live in. Today reality is on the side of death. We try to work in the opposite direction, towards life.

I think it's important to underline the political dimension of the seminar. I mean politics in the poetic sense, not party politics. For me, politics is a question of morals, of saving life. It involves a certain way of looking at texts, of listening to the other. Texts are not just things, dead leaves. They bear witness to life. Reading a text represents a desire to rediscover the human, something which in our world today we tend to forget. In the seminar, we undertake this work of memory, this search for things forgotten, no longer known.

Hélène Cixous: One thing I've discovered just by being alive is that there is truth, and that it's the same everywhere. This might seem obvious, but it's essential. Life has its secrets and they are always the same, but they have to be rediscovered. Truth has to be worked for. Everyone has to rediscover truth and this truth tells itself differently. It tells itself according to each individual biography, each memory and experience.

In the seminar we work on all the different versions of truth. When we read Clarice Lispector, or Genet, or Kafka, we discover that fundamentally they have sensed the same thing. Through a different body, through a different history, and by giving their experiences a different form. The form adds something. It's the contribution every artist and every human being makes to the general treasure of humanity.

But though work on the form is necessary, it doesn't uncover the heart of a text. Hofmannsthal, Clarice Lispector, Genet, Kafka, are as different from each other as it's possible to be and yet they all share the revelation which I believe to be the core of human experience: the nature of the relationship to the other. What Genet calls the theory of equivalences. In different ways, their texts express this revelation.

Nadia Setti: The first of Hélène's texts I read was *La*. I was a student of literary semiotics in Italy at the time and I began reading with all the theoretical baggage I had acquired as a result of my studies. The result was a total failure, because I realized that the theoretical grid I tried to apply was both too generalized and too rigid: it cut me off from the text. The text was free and mobile and escaped all the cages I tried to plaster it with and I felt: delivered. It was as if a door had given me access to a country whose contours were new to me. And instead of worrying about measuring their limits, I felt exhilarated.

Hélène Cixous: We are not outside theory in the seminar though I hope in a way we are above it. We use theoretical instruments, but we use them as aids, as a means of advancing further. This is not a way of repressing or obliterating theory but of giving it a place which is not an end in itself. What I most try to avoid is the turning of theory into an idol. We are not idolaters though neither are we ignorant. We have all undergone our programme of systematic theoretical initiation, but we have done this not to be confined by theory, but for theory to appear as what it is, useful and traversable.

Some years ago there was such an inflation of theoretical discourse in France that whole generations of students were arriving at university already terrorized by the monster. So much so that it was necessary to embark on a programme of theory just to prove to them that it wasn't a monster, but a discourse constituted amongst others which could help us get closer to the text. The problem was that theory was constituted within the institution as an end in itself, like a trophy. We have had to do battle against that.

The theoretical trend in France has been a negative criticism of meaning and representation. A text is neither representation nor expression. A text is beyond both representation — the exact reproduction of reality — and expression: it always says something other than it intends to say. The text is always more than the author wants to express or believes s/he expresses. As a result of fashionable theoretical practices, all this has been repressed. We have been in the phase of non-meaning, in the suspension, the exclusion of the message. This has had serious implications for reading in France. We began to read texts on a purely formal level. University practice is still very largely formal.

Fifteen years ago, Freud was prohibited in feminist circles, on the pretext that he was a misogynist. At the time I wondered how these feminists could possibly hope to get through life because everything had been invented by men. It was like saying, 'we can't go by plane because a woman didn't invent it'. Freud focused attention on the unconscious in an extraordinary series of discoveries. Do we behave as if the unconscious doesn't exist? We live in a post-Freudian, Derridean age of electricity and the aeroplane. So let's do as modern people do, let's use the contemporary means of transport. We owe Freud the exploration of the unconscious.

Freud learnt from the poets. In the network of relays, apprenticeships and schools, we need to know how to give everyone their place. Some of the poets we work on in the seminar didn't know about psychoanalysis, which doesn't stop them from being subject to psychoanalysis. At the same time, in their creation they are poetically beyond psychoanalysis. It's this 'poetically beyond' which is important to me. In the early stages of reading, we go much faster if we are in the analytic automobile, if we take Freud's plane. And we need to go quickly. We need to go quicker to begin with in order to go more slowly later on, to be able to take the time to meditate on the 'poetically beyond' which psychoanalysis can't deal with, philosophy can't deal with, because it escapes them, is stronger, more difficult, more complex, more alive.

Pierre Salesne: In the early days of the seminar, we worked more closely with theoretical texts. They allowed us to overcome certain obstacles, especially in relation to Freud's work. I think that at that time, it was necessary for us to work on theory to undo in ourselves a certain fantasy of mastery, deconstructing what could otherwise become law and prevent us from getting close to the text. I also think it was in relation to what was happening around us. The seminar has never been outside history. We needed to go back over certain texts in order to reply to the weight of theoretical discourse which threatened the work we were trying to do.

Mara Négron Marreo: In Puerto Rico, literature students are trained in American and European theories of textual analysis. The desire to approach the text as an object characterizes most of these theories. One does a job of dissection on the text. Once all the parts are separated, no one knows how to re-assemble them. We forget that at the beginning there was beginning, a living source. The beating heart of the text is cut open on the operating table. The pulse is silenced.

Sarah Cornell: As far as theory is concerned, we do make use of theoretical tools from the fields of literary criticism, psychoanalysis, linguistics and philosophy, but we don't attempt to reduce the texts in order to make them fit into a so-called academic method or into the fixed framework of any given ideological system. In other words, we wouldn't want to attack the text with theoretical swords and daggers. Instead of keeping the text at a distance or burying it under a discourse of mastery, I'd say we try to approach it, not only with our minds, but also with our hearts and souls, trying to hear, and then say, what the text says to us.

Hélène Cixous: The space we work in qualifies itself by the grouping together of many strangenesses. The texts we work on are strange either because of their language or because of what they say. What binds us together is our belief in the need to ensure that the essence of each strangeness is preserved.

The image this meeting of strangenesses evokes for me is one of movement. When I first encountered the texts of Clarice Lispector I remembered Celan's image of the bottle and the sea: the poem's journey to the reader. Reading Clarice, I witnessed this journey. I saw the map of the world crossed by a voice, a message.

Sometimes in the seminar I feel as if we were replying to the curse of Babel. The biblical curse was finding oneself prey to a multiplicity of languages but I see it as a blessing to be in the midst of so many languages. For languages say different things. And our multiple collectivity makes these differences — this infinite enrichment — apparent to us.

There is a passage in Blanchot where the narrator says 'I espoused him in his language'. What we try to do is to espouse a text in its language. When we translate a text, for example, we don't try to *reduce* it to French. We work to preserve the essence of each different language as it passes from one language to the other.

The work we do is a work of love, comparable to the work of love that can take place between two human beings. To understand the other, it is necessary to go in their language, to make the journey through the other's imaginary. For you are strange to me. In the effort to understand, I bring you back to me, compare you to me. I translate you in me. And what I note is your difference, your strangeness. At that moment, perhaps, through recognition of my own differences, I might perceive something of you.

This movement is like a voyage. Sometimes I have worked on countries poetically. Cambodia is an example. In my mind, I had an imaginary Cambodia composed of everything I had read. But, of course, nothing could render the actual experience of going to Cambodia which is something that passes through the body, through the senses, something which happens between Cambodia and me — my encounter with its smell, its space, the colours of its sky.

I have always thought how much I should like to be able to keep all the various stages of this journey. The pre-journey; the imaginary journey. All the preparations for the journey. The first encounter. The moment of discovery. Then everything we bring back from the encounter.

All these different stages are, in reality, the history of a text. And our reading must be a movement capable of following all the stages of this vast journey from one to the other, to me, to you.

I believe that in order to read — to translate — well, we have to undertake this journey ourselves. We have to go to the country of the text and bring back the earth of which the language is made. And every aspect is important, including the things we don't know, the things we discover.

Sarah Cornell: The etymology of 'to translate' tells us a great deal about what translation actually does. 'Translate' comes from the Latin word *translatus* which is the past participle of *transferre* meaning 'to transfer' or 'to translate'. *Ferre* also gives the idea of 'to carry'. Translation is in fact this process of transferring or carrying across. It creates a bridge from one language to another and thus opens a passageway towards the encounter of the other where he or she dwells, speaks, cries or sings in a different tongue.

Violette Santellani: As a result of participating in the seminar, reading has become a new act. Now when I read, I have the impression of slowing down, of changing down to a lower gear. I am still looking at the text as a place of potential self-discovery, but now I am able to reject earlier positions of evasion and identification to enter the body of the text. The image that comes to mind is that of a mouse exploring all the various threads of a text, examining the different colours and knots of meaning, the patterns and designs, all the dark, shadowy creases and folds.

Sarah Cornell: For me, reading is a flowing process of exchange between the reader and the text. On the one hand, reading means working with the text where the text itself is working consciously or unconsciously. On the other hand, as Hélène wrote in 'Approach to Clarice Lispector',[1] reading is 'letting oneself be read' by the text.

Reading in this way calls for the acceptance of a certain position of non-mastery in order to let oneself go towards the mystery or the unknown in the text. However, I think it's important to point out that 'non-mastery' doesn't mean a total lack of orientation nor a failure to recognize the value of modern theory.

Hélène Cixous: Everything begins with love. If we work on a text we don't love, we are automatically at the wrong distance. This happens in many institutions where, in general, one works on a text as if it were an object, using theoretical instruments. It's perfectly possible to make a machine out of the text, to treat it like a machine and be treated by it like a machine. The contemporary tendency has been to find theoretical instruments, a reading technique which has bridled the text, mastered it like a wild horse with saddle and bridle, enslaving it. I am wary of formalist approaches, those which cut up structure, which impose their systematic grid.

If I set loving the text as a condition, I also set up the possibility that there will be people who will not love some of the text we work on.

Some of us won't 'bite' into certain texts, certain texts won't mean anything to us. It doesn't matter. Others amongst us will be called by them and moved to reply.

There are thirty ways into a text. Reading together in this way we bring the text into play. We take a page and everyone comes individually towards it. The text begins to radiate from these approaches. Slowly, we penetrate together to its heart.

I choose to work on the texts that 'touch' me. I use the word deliberately because I believe there is a bodily relationship between reader and text. We work very close to the text, as close to the body of the text as possible; we work phonically, listening to the text, as well as graphically and typographically.

Sometimes I look at the design, the geography of the text, as if it were a map, embodying the world. I look at its legs, its thighs, its belly, as well as its trees and rivers: an immense human and earthly cosmos. I like to work like an ant, crawling the entire length of a text and examining all its details, as well as like a bird that flies over it, or like one of Tsvetaeva's immense ears, listening to its music.

We listen to a text with numerous ears. We hear each other talking with foreign accents and we listen to the foreign accents in the text. Every text has its foreign accents, its strangenesses, and these act like signals, attracting our attention. These strangenesses are our cue. We aren't looking for the author as much as what made the author take the particular path they took, write what they wrote. We're looking for the secret of creation, the same process of creation each one of us is constantly involved with in the process of our lives. Texts are the witnesses of our proceeding. The text opens up a path which is already ours and yet not altogether ours.

Mairéad Hanrahan: In the seminar the text is always worked on in relation to life. Working on the text we try to understand what/who can have produced it, we try to read its making in the traces of its source. So there is a real going over to the other. And what I especially enjoy is the way this faithfulness to the other requires a very close reading of the text, a word by word reading. Each word, each alinea, each comma assumes its meaning. In fact, it is this combination of faithfulness and rigour which I find so valuable in the seminar — a combination which truly enables a reading to bring the text alive.

Regina de Oliveira Machado: I first read Hélène's 'The laugh of the Medusa' as a university undergraduate in Brazil. In this text, questions of femininity were posed which weren't caught where the feminist groups I had been involved in were caught, in a war of sexual opposition. Later I read the continuation of 'The laugh of the Medusa', which is the story of Antony and Cleopatra, in *La Jeune Née*. What I found so extraordinary was that the person reading was sometimes Antony, sometimes Cleopatra. The author was trying to understand and to read the characters from inside, from the point of view of their differences.

Sarah Cornell: The research in the seminar originates from questions concerning writing and sexual difference and they constitute the initial common basis of our work together. Then as different individual questions arise, they engender each person's desire to direct his or her reading in a particular way. The proposed reading list for the year is always extensive and diversified and thus provides an unlimited number of potential paths to be taken. Most of this reading produces work projects which are then presented orally in the seminar. It's always interesting to notice how different these presentations can be in style, in form, as well as in content. On one level, we can follow the research work concerning the text, but on another level, we can also hear the specific questioning and searching of the person speaking.

Hélène Cixous: Some years ago, at the height of the feminist campaigns, a number of women came to the seminar who asked me why there were texts on the annual programme by men. These women had been expecting an exclusively 'feminist' programme with texts written only by women. There has never been in the seminar opposition to or exclusion of one genre by another, one sex by the other.

We work on the mystery of human being, including the fact that humans are sexed beings, that there is sexual difference, and that these differences manifest themselves, write themselves in texts. The differences inscribe themselves in whatever is born from us.

Throughout the world there are differences. Differences of behaviour, differences in relation to living. There are choices. We have a preference for one way of behaviour rather than another because it allows us to live more fully, makes us happier. I prefer a behaviour which is capable of change, capable of taking risks, to a behaviour which is closed and conservative, and which resists any form of loss.

In our work, we are motivated by the inscription of these differences which cannot be contained by the labels man/woman, masculine/feminine. Difference transcends, it traverses everything that exists. It moves in a complex way through every expression, every creation, every (textual) production.

The title of last year's seminar was 'Bereavement and Benediction'. In our reading we traced the theme of bereavement, of how one mourns, how each individual goes through the process of mourning, the apprenticeship that the experience of bereavement represents from earliest childhood through all the stages of life. There is the baby's bereavement, the bereavement of severance, which is also severance for the mother. There are all the stages, all the transformations of the ordeal of bereavement and separation which we encounter in diverse forms throughout life. How do we live the ordeal? What do we make of it? Do we experience it as something negative or do we transform it into something positive? What does it give to writing? These are the questions we work on which we divide for the sake of convenience into 'masculine' and 'feminine'.

For it happens that these questions join with other questions. The distinction between masculine cultural behaviour and feminine cultural behaviour, for example. These questions are the clichés of our time and hold everyone prisoner. Culturally the people whose apprenticeship to bereavement has created a relationship to it which is open and will allow for progress are women. This is because, culturally, women have been taught how to lose, they've been sent to the school of losing. But there are men who have learnt how to lose, who have been to the school of losing and who have come out victorious, transforming their loss into blessing. Some of them are our greatest poets. It's not a question of sex. It's a question of apprenticeship. Which school did you go to?

This year we have worked on texts which are wonderful songs, hymns of what there may be of beauty in the encounter with an inflicted bereavement. We have worked on Mandelstam, on Celan. What do we do when we lose the world, when language is stolen from us by a political regime, when we no longer have a country, when exile is our home? Both men and women have given us their answer.

It's true that I privilege what I would hope to be my answer. I would hope that even in the most extreme exile there will be a force greater than everything, a force which continues to sing: what Celan calls the *Singbarrest*, the singable remains. Even when there is nothing left but silence or the murmuring of despair, I believe there is still hope. Reading Etty Hillesum's diaries from inside the Nazi concentration camps, I am strengthened in my hope. There are texts which help us to believe.

This is where difference leads us. Even though the text carries in its body, in its flesh, the marks of the gender granted us at birth, it necessarily situates itself above these questions.

I don't believe a man and a woman are identical. The fact that men and women have the whole of humanity in common and that at the same time there is something slightly different, I consider a benediction. Our differences have to do with the way we experience pleasure, with our bodily experiences, which are not the same. Our different experiences necessarily leave different marks, different memories. The way we make love — because it isn't the same — produces different sensations and recollections. And these are transmitted through the text. I don't understand what people mean when they tell me these differences don't exist. I consider their belief censorious, repressive, deadly.

These differences are simply a small part of the entirety of a human being.

As a writer, I regret that we cannot go from one side to the other, from one body to another. I regret not being Tiresias. In ancient times, Tiresias was possible. Perhaps he will be again. But I'm not Tiresias. I can write about feminine pleasure, but I can't write about the masculine experience of it. There is a block.

I am not Tiresias. I am not God. I am only a woman, which is already a great deal. From the moment I say: 'I am only a woman', this reserve or opening, inscribes itself in my text. This is the point I write from. It makes itself read. It doesn't run through everything because I'm also a human being. As Clarice Lispector says: 'I'm a woman, plus something else'. A part of me is specifically woman and the rest of me is human. It's the same for a man. These are the backgrounds of inscription, of thinking in the text, which are distinguishable from each other.

If I were to write a historical novel, what would it matter if I were a man or a woman? But if I write about love, then it does matter. I write differently. If I write letting something of my body come through, then this will be different, depending on whether I have experience of a feminine or masculine body.

I could write a thesis on the theme of giving birth in texts by women, it would be fascinating. It's a metaphor which comes easily to women, dictated by their experience. It's a metaphor Clarice Lispector uses, it's a metaphor I use. During childbirth a discovery is made inside the body. We can transpose the discovery, using it to understand moments in life which are analogous. A man will understand different things differently. Their bodies are sources of totally different images, transformations, expressions.

Violette Santellani: Before the experience of working in the seminar where the majority of the participants are women, I felt alienated, at one remove from the text. It was only through working with other women that I discovered that it is possible to be both mind and body, without a split, and without the inevitable loss of memory. And I derived an immense source of support — of self-confirmation — from this experience, which my daily life, with its stereotypes and its interdictions, had always denied.

Ever since I was a child I have longed for texts which would preserve all the attributes of femininity. Now in the seminar, I search with both sexes for a way of living this inscription in a phallocentric world where, each day, the false values put out by the medias threaten this truth, this experience, this desire.

Hélène Cixous: Language is a translation. It speaks through the body.

Each time we translate what we are in the process of thinking, it necessarily passes through our bodies. If a woman disposes of her body (and I'm not talking about women who are alienated from their bodies, but about those who have a body which is theirs, who inhabit it, live in it), when she speaks, her words pass through it. This gives another universe of expression from men. We are not machines.

People often ask me: are there any great writers? It's a question I always have difficulty with because, of course, there are great writers: great technicians, great artists of writing, extraordinary acrobats of language. But I believe in the importance of the message in a text. Writers only begin to interest me if what they say has a relationship to humanity.

I believe the text should establish an ethical relation to reality as well as to artistic practice. I might summarize my definition of poetry as 'philosophic singing'. Philosophic reasoning, and, at the same time, the overflowing of the boundaries of philosophic discourse; making the river of poetry flow into the bed of philosophy. Some poetry, of course, doesn't have a message. There is poetry which is more musical than thoughtful. What I call poetry crosses the fertile field of philosophy in order to go beyond.

A few years ago, we subtitled our work in the seminar with the doublet 'poetry-politics'. This was in the attempt not to let poetry stray too far from reality, in the struggle to try to think politically via a poetic route.

As far as my own writing is concerned, my constant worry has been to try to find a footbridge, a way of crossing from a world so totally anti-poetic as the world of political actuality to a world of poetry. To ensure the bridge isn't cut. And very often I have had the feeling that all I can do is to note the difficulty, the virtual impossibility of passage. There were echoes, recollections of one world by the other, but I had difficulty finding the crossings.

History gives us lessons. The texts of Mandelstam, Celan, all those who were involved in violent political conflict, who were imprisoned in the concentration camps, are bearers of texts, suffering, heavy, impregnated with political reality.

But I don't believe we can play with the facts. Someone who has not been in a concentration camp cannot say what someone who has been imprisoned says. But one thing we who have escaped the camps can do is to make the effort to turn our thoughts towards those who are in captivity. The other thing is to try to find a language that corresponds to the reality of the camps.

This is a question which has haunted me. In every one of my texts, through the troubles in Vietnam, Iran, the USSR — the list is endless — my question has been: how can we talk about it? Can we talk about it? Who has the right to talk about it? What form must our talking about it take? What form can we give to our outrage, speaking about these things which are unspeakable, which take away our breath?

One way is by inscribing the question, signifying our impotence, our obligation, our memory of what is happening.

Personally, I found the only way I could deal with politics — poetically — was by changing genres.

Reading *The Hour of the Star* I realized what a revolution Clarice Lispector underwent in order to get close to the other. In *The Hour of the Star* Clarice Lispector asks the question of how to talk of the other, how to leave space for the other: how to create the other's space. And to answer her question, she literally transformed herself to the point of changing roles, changing sex.

Sometimes, in fiction, the answers are extreme. Because the other in these cases is extreme. I have only been able to resolve the question in an equivalent movement to Clarice's strategy which consists in making the author I am fade to the point of disappearing. I, the author, have to disappear so that you, so other, can appear. My answer has come through writing for the theatre.

On the stage, I, the author, am no longer there, but there is the other. And even the absolute other, the absolute stranger.

The author's 'I' should be the lightest, the most transparent possible. I don't believe that this is a point we arrive at straight away. The inaugural gesture of writing is always in a necessary relation to narcissism. When one begins to write, one is constantly reminding oneself of the fact: 'I write'. Rimbaud is a good example, his verse echoes with 'I', 'I', 'I' . . . an absolutely magnificent, exploded 'I'. It takes time for 'I' to get used to 'I'. Time for the 'I' to be sure 'I' exists. Only then is there room for the other.

My work now is child of the theatre, product of the theatre, but I have had to go through all the various stages to come to this point. I have had to change genres and I've only been able to do that through working on the 'I'. And the work has taken time.

Perhaps 200 years ago, I would have written fiction like Kleist. Kleist is theatrical. His fiction presents a stage. There is an agreement between the text and the reader which is comparable to the one that exists between the play and the public. We open the text and the play begins. That's how it's written. With a total withdrawal of the author. But we can no longer write like Kleist. We no longer live in Kleist's time. We can't write now as people wrote then. We can't write in the age of the aeroplane as people wrote 200 years ago. We are in the age of the unconscious, of linguistic transformation. We could try to copy Kleist, of course, but if we did, what we wrote would be a reconstruction. Now that we have another language, we can't go backwards. We cannot rewrite the Bible as it has been written.

We always say the same thing. What changes is our way of saying it. A new effect is produced by the shift, the alteration in form.

This is what Clarice Lispector says in her story about love. We have loved in the same way ever since the world existed. And yet, of course, it's completely different because everyone reinvents their own version. The same is true of the text. When I read, what moves me is the finding of a new image, a new way of saying the most ancient and eternal truths. It's this novelty of expression which is extraordinary and which pays tribute to the incredible richness of the human imagination.

Note

1. 'Approche de Clarice Lispector', *Poetique*, No. 40, Paris, Editions du Seuil, November 1979, p. 407.

Selected further reading

(English editions and translations have been given wherever possible.)
The Bible.
KAREN BLIXEN, (ISAK DINESEN), *Out of Africa, Winter's Tales*, both published in Penguin Modern Classics, Harmondsworth, Penguin, 1954 and 1983.
PAUL CELAN, *Paul Celan: Poems*, a bilingual edition, selected, translated and introduced by Michael Hamburger, Manchester, Carcanet, 1980.
JACQUES DERRIDA, *De la Grammotologie*, Paris, Editions de Minuit, 1967, translated by Gayatri Spivak as *Of Grammatology*, Baltimore, John Hopkins University Press, 1967; *L'Ecriture et la Différence*, Paris, Editions de Seuil, 1967, translated by Alan Bass as *Writing and Difference*, London, Routledge and Kegan Paul, 1978; *Marges de la philosophie*, Paris, Editions de Minuit, 1972, translated by Alan Bass as *Margins of Philosophy*, Brighton, Harvester, 1982; *La Voix et le phénomène*, Paris, Presses Universitaires de France, 1972, translated by David B. Allison as *Speech and Phenomena*, Evanston, Illinois, Northwestern University Press, 1973; *Spurs: Nietzsche's Styles/Eperons: les styles de Nietzsche*, a bilingual edition translated by Barbara Harlow, Chicago, University of Chicago Press, 1978; *La Carte postale de Socrate à Freud et au-delà*, Paris, Flammarion, 1980.
FEDOR MIKHAILOVICH DOSTOIEVSKI, *The Brothers Karamazov, The Idiot*, both translated for the Penguin Classics by David Magarshack, Harmondsworth, Penguin, 1958 and 1955.

SIGMUND FREUD, *The Standard Edition of the Complete Psychological Works of Sigmund Freud*, edited by James Strachey in 24 volumes, London, Hogarth Press, 1953–74, especially *Five Lectures on Psycho-Analysis, The Interpretation of Dreams*, and *On Sexuality*.

GEORG WILHELM FRIEDRICH HEGEL, *The Phenomenology of Mind*, translated by J. B. Baillie, London, Allen and Unwin, 1931.

MARTIN HEIDEGGER, *On the Way to Language*, translated by Peter D. Hertz, London, Harper and Row, 1971; a useful introduction in English to Heidegger's work is *Poetry, Language, Thought*, introduced and translated by Albert Hofstadter, New York, Harper Colophon Books, Harper and Row, 1975.

HERMANN HESSE, *Journey to the East*, translated by Hilda Rosner, London, Peter Owen, 1964; *Narcissus and Goldmund*, translated by Ursule Molinaro, New York, Bantam Books, 1971.

FRANZ KAFKA, *Letters to Felice*, (Correspondence with Felice Bauer), edited by Erich Heller and Jürgen Born and translated by James Stern and Elisabeth Duckworth, London, Secker and Warburg, 1974; *Letters to Milena*, (Correspondence with Milena Jesenka-Polak), edited by Will Haas and translated by Tania and James Stern, London, Secker and Warburg, 1953; *Wedding Preparations in the Country (and other posthumous prose writings)*, translated by Ernst Kaiser and Eithe Wilkins, London, Secker and Warburg, 1954.

SOREN KIERKEGAARD, *Fear and Trembling*, translated by Walter Lowrie, Princeton, Princeton University Press, 1954.

HEINRICH VON KLEIST, 'The Earthquake in Chile', 'The Marquise of O' and 'Michael Kohlaas', in *the Marquise of O and Other Stories*, Penguin Modern Classics, Harmondsworth, Penguin, 1978.

MARCEL MAUSS, 'Essai sur le don. Forme et raison de l'échange dans les sociétés archaïques', in *Sociologie et Anthropologie*, Paris, Presses Universitaires de France, 1950.

RAINER MARIA RILKE, *The Notebooks of Malte Laurids Brigge*, translated by Stephen Mitchell, New York, Random House, 1983; *Sonnets to Orpheus*, a bilingual edition translated by J. B. Leishman, London, Hogarth Press, 1936.

WILLIAM SHAKESPEARE, *King Lear*.

MARINA TSVETAEVA, *Selected Poems*, translated by Elaine Feinstein, Oxford, Oxford University Press, 1981.

Books by Hélène Cixous

1967   *Le Prénom de Dieu*, Paris, Grasset.
1969   *Dedans*, Paris, Grasset.
—   *L'Exil ou l'art du remplacement*, Paris, Grasset, translated into
            English by Sally Purcell, as *The Exile of James Joyce*, London,
            John Calder, 1972.
1970   *Le Troisième Corps*, Paris, Grasset.
—   *Les Commencements*, Paris, Grasset.
1971   *La Pupille*, Paris, Cahiers Renaud-Barrault.
—   *Un Vrai Jardin*, Paris, L'Herne.
1972   *Neutre*, Paris, Grasset.
1973   *Tombe*, Paris, Editions de Seuil.
1974   *Prénoms de personne*, Paris, Editions de Seuil.
—   *Portrait du soleil*, Paris, Denoël.
1975   *Révolutions pour plus d'un Faust*, Paris, Editions de Seuil.
—   *La Jeune Née*, in collaboration with Catherine Clément, Paris,
            Union Générale d'Editions, Collection 10/18, translated into
            English by Betsy Wing as *The Newly Born Woman*, Manchester,
            Manchester University Press, 1986.
—   *Un K. incompréhensible: Pierre Goldman*, Paris, Christian Bourgois.
—   *Souffles*, Paris, Editions des femmes.
1976   *Portrait de Dora*, Paris, Editions des femmes.
—   *La*, Paris, Gallimard.
—   *Partie*, Paris, Editions des femmes.

1977   *La Venue à l'écriture*, with Catherine Clément and Madeleine Gagnon, Paris, Union Générale d'Editions, Collection 10/18.

—   *Angst*, Paris, Editions des femmes, translated into English by Jo Levy, London, John Calder, 1985.

1978   *Préparatifs de noces au delà de l'abîme*, Paris, Editions des femmes.

—   *Chant du corps interdit/Le Nom d'Oedipe*, Paris, Editions des femmes.

1979   *Vivre l'orange*, Paris, Editions des femmes.

—   *Anankè*, Paris, Editions des femmes.

1980   *Illa*, Paris, Editions des femmes.

1981   *Ou l'art de l'innocence*, Paris, Editions des femmes.

1982   *Limonade tout était si infini*, Paris, Editions des femmes.

1983   *Le Livre de Promethea*, Paris, Gallimard.

1984   *La Prise de l'école de Madubaï*, Paris, Avant-scène.

1985   *L'Histoire terrible mais inachevée de Norodom Sihanouk roi du Cambodge*, Paris, Théâtre du Soleil.

1986   *La Bataille d'Arcachon*, Editions Trois, Québec, Laval.

—   *Entre l'écriture*, Paris, Editions des femmes.

Hélène Cixous' play, *L'Indiade ou l'Inde de leurs rêves* will be published in French and in an English translation in 1988.

Two translated volumes of transcripts from the seminar are also scheduled for publication by the University of Minnesota Press (Verena Conley editor) in 1988.